Creative Arts

The HighScope Preschool Curriculum

Creative Arts

Ann S. Epstein, PhD

HIGHSCOPE®

Published by
HighScope® Press

A division of the
HighScope Educational Research Foundation
600 North River Street
Ypsilanti, Michigan 48198-2898
734.485.2000, FAX 734.485.0704
Orders: 800.40.PRESS; Fax: 800.442.4FAX; www.highscope.org
E-mail: *press@highscope.org*

Editor: Jennifer Burd
Cover design, text design: Judy Seling, Seling Design LLC
Production: Judy Seling, Seling Design LLC; Kazuko Sacks, Profit Makers LLC
Photography:
Bob Foran — front cover, 8, 9, 17, 20, 22 (top), 24 (top left), 25, 30, 31, 47, 64, 67, 68, 70, 72, 77, 81, 82, 89, back cover (left)
Gregory Fox — 1, 4, 7, 13, 14, 15, 18, 19, 22 (bottom), 23, 24 (top and bottom right), 28, 36, 37, 41, 42, 43, 45, 49, 53, 57, 58, 59, 62, 63, 65, 76, 83, 86, 88, 93, back cover (right)
Pat Thompson — 33

Library of Congress Cataloging-in-Publication Data
Epstein, Ann S.
Creative arts / Ann S. Epstein, PhD.
pages cm. -- (The HighScope preschool curriculum)
Includes bibliographical references.
ISBN 978-1-57379-656-9 (soft cover : alk. paper) 1. Arts--Study and teaching (Preschool) 2. Arts--Curricula. I. Title.
LB1140.5.A7E68 2012
372.5--dc23

2012003701

Printed in the United States of America
10 9 8 7 6

Contents

Acknowledgments

Many people contributed their knowledge and skills to the publication of *Creative Arts*. I want to thank the early childhood and other staff members who collaborated on creating the key developmental indicators (KDIs) in this content area: Beth Marshall, Sue Gainsley, Shannon Lockhart, Polly Neill, Kay Rush, Julie Hoelscher, Emily Thompson, and Karen Sawyers. Among this group of colleagues, those who devoted special attention to reviewing the manuscript for this book were Kay Rush, Beth Marshall, and Karen Sawyers. Mary Hohmann, whose expertise informs many other HighScope curriculum books, also provided detailed feedback.

The developmental scaffolding charts in this volume — describing what children might do and say and how adults can support and gently extend their learning at different developmental levels — are invaluable contributions to the curriculum. I am grateful to Beth Marshall and Sue Gainsley for the extraordinary working relationship we forged in creating these charts. By bringing our unique experiences to this challenging process, we integrated knowledge about child development and effective classroom practices from the perspectives of research, teaching, training, and policy.

Thanks are also due to Nancy Brickman, who directed the editing and production of the book. I extend particular appreciation to Jennifer Burd, who edited the volume, and Katie Bruckner, who assisted with all aspects of the publication process. I also want to acknowledge the following individuals for contributing to the book's visual appeal and reader friendliness: photographers Bob Foran and Gregory Fox, and graphic artists Judy Seling (book designer) and Kazuko Sacks (book production).

Finally, I extend sincerest thanks to all the teachers, trainers, children, and families whose participation in HighScope and other early childhood programs has contributed to the creation and authenticity of the HighScope Preschool Curriculum over the decades. I hope this book continues to support their exploration and learning in the creative arts for many years to come.

CHAPTER 1

The Importance of Creative Arts

What Are the Creative Arts?

The **creative arts** call upon many other areas of development. Children express their feelings, use words and body language to communicate their ideas, draw and build props to support their pretend play, act out family and community roles, document their own artistic ideas, and reflect on what artists are saying and the materials and tools they use to get their message across.

Important perceptual, cognitive, and social-emotional changes during the preschool years support the development of the creative arts. Chief among these is the growing ability to hold mental images in mind and represent them by drawing and making models, singing songs and creating movements, and pretending to be real and imaginary characters. Using all their senses and emerging thought processes, young children are capable of both making and appreciating art.

The creative arts in early education include visual art, music, movement, and pretend play. Artistic expression engages children's intellect and emotions, as well as their physical and social skills. In short, the arts are valuable when explored on their own, and they also promote discovery when integrated with other areas of the curriculum. The creative arts open the door to learning about oneself and others, encourage experimentation and reflection, and enrich our lives. Moreover, because children learn in multiple ways, the arts provide a venue to "reflect these multiple ways of knowing and doing" (Arts Education Partnership, 1998, p. 4). Preschool presents many opportunities to engage young children in the exploration and enjoyment of the arts.

The creative arts have been a standard feature of early childhood programs since their beginning. Curriculum writer Carol Seefeldt (1999) observed that even during periods when educators are pressured to focus on academic

Creative Arts in Action

At planning time, Quentin draws two bodies with arms, legs, neck, face, hair, eyes, nose, and mouth. "This is me and this is Balta," he says. "We're going to work in the block area."

❖

At large-group time, Holly alternately taps her knees and shoulders with rhythm sticks to the steady beat of "Row, Row, Row Your Boat."

❖

At large-group time, Luke twirls his ribbon to the slow music. "I'm moving like a jellyfish," he says to his teacher Linda.

❖

At work time at the sand and water table, Forrest sings "underwater fire truck, underwater fire truck" as he submerges his truck. "Into the water it goes," he sings.

❖

At work time in the house area, three children pretend together. "First I'm a bad guy. Then I'm going to be a prince," says Evan. "He's going to steal my crown," says Zoe, the princess. "Hey Evan," adds Yasmina, "How about you come and find me, then you steal the crown?"

❖

At work time in the art area, Wendy chooses the purple marker. She says to her teacher Tanya, "I like purple. It's my favorite color because it is dark and light."

skills, such as reading, most continue to believe that the arts are an essential component of the curriculum in preschool and the early grades. In the introduction to the National Association for the Education of Young Children's (NAEYC's) *Spotlight on Young Children and the Creative Arts*, Derry Koralek (2005) says:

> The arts invite children to imagine, solve problems, express ideas and emotions, and make sense of their experiences. Creative arts are a meaningful part of the early childhood curriculum for their own sake and because they can enhance children's development of skills in literacy, science, mathematics, social studies, and more. (p. 2)

Research supports this enduring belief in the educational value of the creative arts. The multisite study *Champions of Change: The Impact of the Arts on Learning* (Fiske, 1999) found that children benefited from arts experiences throughout their school years. The gains they made in cognitive, linguistic, and social development during arts-based activities transferred to virtually every other domain of learning. American educators are increasingly concerned that children are losing their creative edge in the single-minded pursuit of academic knowledge. Advocates for arts education stress that it is not an either/or choice. "Researchers say creativity should be taken out of the art room and put into homeroom. The argument that we can't teach creativity because kids already have too much to learn is a false trade-off. Creativity isn't about freedom from facts. Rather, fact-finding and deep research are vital stages in the creative process" (Bronson & Merryman, 2010, para. 11).

> "Humans have always used the arts to share and make sense of their deepest joys and fears. When we bring the shadows out of the caves and turn them into story, dance, song, or picture, we transform our emotions into something to share with others. And on those rare days when all the planets are perfectly aligned, we react in ways that lead to a greater understanding for all."
>
> — Matlock & Hornstein (2005, pp. 7–8)

In addition to providing appropriate materials and opportunities to explore the creative arts, the most important gift adults can provide is a safe and secure setting in which children feel free to express themselves artistically. A nurturing environment allows Quentin to make a detailed drawing; Holly to feel the steady beat of a familiar tune; Luke to move creatively to music and Forrest to create a song; Evan, Zoe, and Yasmina to engage together in complex role play; and Wendy to voice an aesthetic preference (see "Creative Arts in Action" on p. 2).

The Intrinsic and Extrinsic Value of the Arts

Proponents of arts education cite its inner and outer rewards. They explain that the arts engage children — and the adults who work with them — both emotionally and intellectually. The arts are *intrinsically rewarding* and therefore an important endeavor in their own right. Children learn to value creative expression in themselves and others, and they derive inner satisfaction from appreciating beauty or wrestling with artistic challenges. Humanities professor Stephen Dobbs says that through arts education, "students begin to see the rich mosaic of the world from many perspectives" (Dobbs, 1998, p. 12). For young children in particular, the creative arts provide an inner sense of competence and control. The Task Force on Children's Learning and the Arts notes that "as they engage in the artistic process, children learn that they can observe, organize, and interpret their experiences. They can make decisions, take actions, and monitor the effect of those actions" (Arts Education Partnership, 1998, p. 2).

The creative arts are also *extrinsically valuable* because they promote learning in other domains. For example, students use spatial relationships when they move to music or strengthen their eye-hand coordination when they weave. Noted art educator Rudolph Arnheim (1989) emphasized that engaging with the arts is as much an intellectual activity as an intuitive one. And, as stressed by the Arts Education Partnership, learning about the creative arts contributes to the development of many social and academic skills. "For all children, at all ability levels, the arts play a central role in cognitive, motor, language, and social-emotional development. The arts motivate and engage children in learning, stimulate memory and facilitate understanding, enhance symbolic communication, promote relationships, and provide an avenue for building competence" (Arts Education Partnership, 1998, p. v).

Artistic Development in Preschool

Developmental changes in the preschool years make children especially open to learning from the opportunities that arts education presents. Preschoolers can form mental images. They are

The arts engage children both intellectually and emotionally; children derive inner satisfaction from engaging in the arts.

less tied to the here-and-now than infants and toddlers and can deal with symbols, draw on memory, and use their imaginations. "Being able to think about something not present and then find a way to express it is a major cognitive accomplishment for young children" (Seefeldt, 1995, p. 40). This ability allows three- and four-year-olds to convey their experiences through various forms of artistic representation. They can paint a picture of their family (art), make up a song about an upcoming birthday party or one that recently took place (music), move like a cloud (movement), or role-play making dinner (pretend play).

At the same time, because young children are also developing their language skills, the arts open up new avenues for expression and communication. As their expanding cognitive and linguistic capacities are combined with their growing physical and social abilities, preschoolers have a wide array of options for both creating and appreciating the arts. They can draw pictures and build models, sing and invent the words to songs, reflect emotions through movement, and imitate and pretend to be real or imaginary characters. In short, young children can do many of the things that adult artists do. However, they do so in ways that are consistent with their developmental levels and abilities.

"Since the introduction of more 'found' and open-ended materials in the classroom, I have seen children blossom into their own creativity. Their artwork is more imaginative. There is a definite increase in the amount of dramatic play, especially in the house and block areas."

— Salt Lake City, Utah, Teacher

Principles of Early Arts Education

Keeping the internal and external benefits of the arts in mind, along with preschoolers' emerging cognitive and language abilities, effective arts education in the early years should be guided by the following four developmental principles:

Representation grows out of children's real experiences

To form mental images, young children first need hands-on experiences with objects, people, and events. For example, when they play "mommy" and "baby," children carry out the roles they typically see in their own families. Their drawings and clay models reflect the people, animals, furniture, and so on seen in their everyday lives, as well as in books and electronic media. Similarly, children's melodies, rhythms, and song topics arise from their musical experiences at home and school. They move their bodies in the ways they observe in parents, siblings, peers, and teachers.

At work time in the art area, Nadia makes a snowman by stacking three balls of play dough. She gets two golf tees from the woodworking area for arms, and uses small beads for eyes.

❖

At work time in the block area, Eva sits in the "car" built by Kyle with a doll in her lap. She says, "My baby threw up. I need to drive her straight to the hospital." Kyle makes a "siren" sound as he pretends to turn a steering wheel. Eva calls over Shannon (a teacher) and says, "Doctor, hurry! Give my baby a checkup and a shot to make her better." Doctor Shannon attends to the "patient" and pronounces her completely healed. Eva directs Kyle to drive them home so she can put the baby to bed. She tells him not to

Stages in Making and Appreciating Art

Stages in Making Art

The stages of artistic development do not have discrete beginnings and endings (Taunton & Colbert, 2000). Children tend to move back and forth within and between levels, somewhat like adults artists do when they work with an unfamiliar medium or explore a new idea. Nevertheless, theory and research do point to four general progressions over time (Epstein & Trimis, 2002):

- ***From accidental or spontaneous representation to intentional representation.*** Only 30% of four-year-olds, compared with 80% of five-year-olds, begin to draw with an intention in mind (Thompson, 1995). Younger children accidentally create a form and then decide it looks like something; for example, they may pat clay into a rectangle and call it a car. This order is later reversed; children start with specific characteristics in mind and find or manipulate materials to match their mental image. This same progression applies to other artistic media. For example, a child may initially roll on the floor and say, "Look, it's a ball!" but later intentionally imitate a ball, saying, "I'm gonna be a ball. I'll bounce up and down and roll on the floor." Of course, at any age or level, found objects, overheard sounds, or accidental movements can inspire creativity.
- ***From simple to elaborated models.*** Initially, children hold one or two salient characteristics in mind and re-create them in drawings, songs, movements, or pretend play. Later, as they are able to hold more attributes in mind, their representations become more detailed. For example, children may at first draw a face as a circle with two dots for eyes. Later, they include other facial features (nose, mouth, ears, eyebrows) as well as hair, a particular facial expression, and perhaps a decoration (a headband or necklace). In a pretend-play scenario, a younger child in the role of a baby may go "Waa! Waa!" in imitation of crying. An older child in the same role might wriggle and make faces, crawl, suck on a bottle, or reach out to be picked up.
- ***From randomness to deliberation.*** When children first explore an art medium, the sheer joy of using motion to make a mark is satisfying, even if it is repeated to the point of leaving a hole in the paper! As they gain more control over the materials and tools, children become more deliberate in the images they create. They begin by making lines, followed by shapes and forms. Drawing an enclosed shape — making a line that changes direction and returns to the starting point — requires visual-motor coordination and intentionality. This development can also be seen in the sounds and movements children make. For example, after initially playing all over the scale with their voices, children will later try to reproduce a specific pitch (note). Likewise, their movements become more refined. Instead of just moving randomly from place to place, children may attempt to move in a circular pattern and return to their starting point.
- ***From unrelated elements to relationships.*** Children become increasingly aware of how marks, sounds, and movements relate to one another. At first, random marks land wherever a child's hand alights. Later, children intentionally place marks in relation to other markings. The same is true of sounds; children sing single notes but later string them together to make a tune. They make a series of unconnected movements, but then deliberately connect one movement to another. Likewise, as children's play scenarios advance, one episode leads more logically to another (from just mixing things in a bowl to "cooking" soup to opening a restaurant that serves soup to customers). In addition to artistic development, these trends also reflect the child's greater interest in representational accuracy, growing spatial awareness, and emerging social skills. Aesthetics also begins to enter into artistic decisions. For example, children place colors or shapes in proximity because they "look pretty next to one another." They sing a series of pitches because "they sound nice together." When children combine artistic actions with aesthetic judgments in this way, making and appreciating art converge.

Stages in Appreciating Art

Stages of art appreciation are often based on the developmental progressions of Jean Piaget and other cognitive theorists (Kerlavage, 1995). For example, for cognitive psychologist M. J. Parsons (1987), art appreciation begins with concrete and personal judgments and ends with abstract and socially developed views about art. Although theorists differ over the specifics, they usually organize children's aesthetic growth according to at least three general levels:

- ***Sensorial.*** The youngest children generally like abstract images and works that appeal to their senses. They respond to bright color contrasts and bold visual patterns, music with a strong beat, movements with a dominant action, and characters with clear personality traits. Children at this stage respond emotionally to art, and may have difficulty explaining the reasons for their preferences. Often, one object, sound, or action catches their attention to the exclusion of other aspects of the work. They may not differentiate between alternative forms of a work of art, for example, between a painting and a sculpture or between a reproduction and a photograph.

- ***Concrete.*** As children develop a sense for symbols, their preferences depend more on subject matter or theme. They like artwork whose ideas they can relate to, portrayed in a simple and realistic manner. Children in this middle stage also develop an initial concept of beauty, again related to whether the subject matter appeals to them. They see the purpose of art as telling a "story" — through image, sound, or action — about real people and events. Children at this stage are also able to sort art by its medium, and they have an understanding of time. They can tell whether visual images, musical styles, or costumes are from long ago, are from the present, or are futuristic.

- ***Expressive.*** By late preschool or early kindergarten, children can begin to think about works of art from the artist's point of view, speculate about what the artist intended, and judge how "good" a work of art is (or is not) based on their response to it (Seefeldt, 1999). They may consciously use an artist's subject matter or technique in their own artwork. While they still prefer realism, children become more interested in subtle colors, complicated compositions, and the expressive feelings behind the artwork. Because they can appreciate other points of view, children in this stage become more aware of different artistic styles. Being able to take different perspectives also attunes them to how personal beliefs and cultural influences affect an artist's work. Taking all these factors into account, children at this stage will defend their preferences in terms of artistic style, expressive qualities, and aesthetic principles.

Children need hands-on experiences with objects, people, and events in order to form mental images and then represent them.

make the siren noise because the baby is sleeping and "she needs her rest so she won't get sick again."

❖

At work time in the house area, Odile pretends to wash her hands in the sink. She shakes the salt shaker with a steady movement against her hands and says it is soap.

❖

At large-group time, Peter puts his hands against the wall, bends his knees, and squats "like my sister Jessica does at ballet class."

Children's representations develop from the simple to the complex

Whatever the artistic medium (painting, singing, moving, acting), children's representations begin simply and evolve in complexity with time and practice. Initially, they hold only one or two characteristics of an object, person, or event in mind. Later, as children are able to store more attributes in their mental images, and become increasingly skillful at using materials and actions to portray them, their representations also become more detailed and elaborate.

At recall time, three-year-old Bridget draws in her recall journal. She makes some marks with crayons and says they are the things she was using in the toy area (the widgets). [One year later:] At recall time, Bridget draws three people and the widgets she uses at work time. She draws the people with legs, arms, bodies, eyes, ears, noses, and hair.

Remember, however, that young children do not move neatly through these stages of artistic development (Taunton & Colbert, 2000). Rather, they shift within levels, especially as they discover an unfamiliar medium or explore a new means of expression. In this respect, children are like adult artists. At all ages, creativity means giving oneself over to play and exploration, and enjoying both the simplicity and complexity that an artistic medium has to offer.

Each child's representations are unique

Children express themselves in ways that make sense to them and that reflect their interests, experiences, and personalities. For example, children's behavior may be silly or intense; their manner may be slapdash or deliberate; and their attitude may show an awareness of their audience or obliviousness to it. Adults should therefore view and respect each child's artistic creations as one of a kind. Children, like adult artists, need the emotional and physical space to create freely in a supportive environment.

Young children are capable of appreciating as well as making art

Educators often think that art appreciation is too abstract or analytical for preschoolers. But because young children are so observant and in tune with all their senses, they are ideal candidates for appreciating the world of art. In fact, they are often eager to share their reactions to a picture, song, dance, or story. The key, says art educator Marjorie Schiller, is that "talking about art should spring from the interests of the children and be initiated, for the most part, by them" (1995, p. 34). It is therefore important to include appreciating as well as making art in the preschool curriculum, grounding both in the experiences that young children find meaningful in their own lives.

Each child's representations are unique.

Preschoolers looked at reproductions of fine artwork on postcards and in books. Then they discussed what they saw and thought about the paintings. They found out that Michelangelo painted on the ceiling, noticed the cracks in old paintings, compared Georgia O'Keefe's canvases to the flowers in their science area, and were surprised to hear that the names of Ninja Turtles were those of real artists. The children instantly recognized that Matisse had a very different style from the realism of Michelangelo and da Vinci (Schiller (1995, p. 37).

Representation grows out of children's real experiences.

Children enjoy and learn from exploring art materials.

HighScope Preschool Curriculum Content

Key Developmental Indicators

A. Approaches to Learning

1. **Initiative**: Children demonstrate initiative as they explore their world.
2. **Planning**: Children make plans and follow through on their intentions.
3. **Engagement**: Children focus on activities that interest them.
4. **Problem solving**: Children solve problems encountered in play.
5. **Use of resources**: Children gather information and formulate ideas about their world.
6. **Reflection**: Children reflect on their experiences.

B. Social and Emotional Development

7. **Self-identity**: Children have a positive self-identity.
8. **Sense of competence**: Children feel they are competent.
9. **Emotions**: Children recognize, label, and regulate their feelings.
10. **Empathy**: Children demonstrate empathy toward others.
11. **Community**: Children participate in the community of the classroom.
12. **Building relationships**: Children build relationships with other children and adults.
13. **Cooperative play**: Children engage in cooperative play.
14. **Moral development**: Children develop an internal sense of right and wrong.
15. **Conflict resolution**: Children resolve social conflicts.

C. Physical Development and Health

16. **Gross-motor skills**: Children demonstrate strength, flexibility, balance, and timing in using their large muscles.
17. **Fine-motor skills**: Children demonstrate dexterity and hand-eye coordination in using their small muscles.
18. **Body awareness**: Children know about their bodies and how to navigate them in space.
19. **Personal care**: Children carry out personal care routines on their own.
20. **Healthy behavior**: Children engage in healthy practices.

D. Language, Literacy, and Communication[1]

21. **Comprehension**: Children understand language.
22. **Speaking**: Children express themselves using language.
23. **Vocabulary**: Children understand and use a variety of words and phrases.
24. **Phonological awareness**: Children identify distinct sounds in spoken language.
25. **Alphabetic knowledge**: Children identify letter names and their sounds.
26. **Reading**: Children read for pleasure and information.
27. **Concepts about print**: Children demonstrate knowledge about environmental print.
28. **Book knowledge**: Children demonstrate knowledge about books.
29. **Writing**: Children write for many different purposes.
30. **English language learning**: (If applicable) Children use English and their home language(s) (including sign language).

---

[1]Language, Literacy, and Communication KDIs 21–29 may be used for the child's home language(s) as well as English. KDI 30 refers specifically to English language learning.

E. Mathematics

31. **Number words and symbols**: Children recognize and use number words and symbols.
32. **Counting**: Children count things.
33. **Part-whole relationships**: Children combine and separate quantities of objects.
34. **Shapes**: Children identify, name, and describe shapes.
35. **Spatial awareness**: Children recognize spatial relationships among people and objects.
36. **Measuring**: Children measure to describe, compare, and order things.
37. **Unit**: Children understand and use the concept of unit.
38. **Patterns**: Children identify, describe, copy, complete, and create patterns.
39. **Data analysis**: Children use information about quantity to draw conclusions, make decisions, and solve problems.

F. Creative Arts

40. **Art**: Children express and represent what they observe, think, imagine, and feel through two- and three-dimensional art.
41. **Music**: Children express and represent what they observe, think, imagine, and feel through music.
42. **Movement**: Children express and represent what they observe, think, imagine, and feel through movement.
43. **Pretend play**: Children express and represent what they observe, think, imagine, and feel through pretend play.
44. **Appreciating the arts**: Children appreciate the creative arts.

G. Science and Technology

45. **Observing**: Children observe the materials and processes in their environment.
46. **Classifying**: Children classify materials, actions, people, and events.
47. **Experimenting**: Children experiment to test their ideas.
48. **Predicting**: Children predict what they expect will happen.
49. **Drawing conclusions**: Children draw conclusions based on their experiences and observations.
50. **Communicating ideas**: Children communicate their ideas about the characteristics of things and how they work.
51. **Natural and physical world**: Children gather knowledge about the natural and physical world.
52. **Tools and technology**: Children explore and use tools and technology.

H. Social Studies

53. **Diversity**: Children understand that people have diverse characteristics, interests, and abilities.
54. **Community roles**: Children recognize that people have different roles and functions in the community.
55. **Decision making**: Children participate in making classroom decisions.
56. **Geography**: Children recognize and interpret features and locations in their environment.
57. **History**: Children understand past, present, and future.
58. **Ecology**: Children understand the importance of taking care of their environment.

About This Book

In the HighScope Preschool Curriculum, the content of children's learning is organized into eight areas: A. Approaches to Learning; B. Social and Emotional Development; C. Physical Development and Health; D. Language, Literacy, and Communication; E. Mathematics; F. Creative Arts; G. Science and Technology; and H. Social Studies. Within each content area, HighScope identifies **key developmental indicators (KDIs)** that are the building blocks of young children's thinking and reasoning.

The term *key developmental indicators* encapsulates HighScope's approach to early education. The word *key* refers to the fact that these are the meaningful ideas children should learn and experience. The second part of the term — *developmental* — conveys the idea that learning is gradual and cumulative. Learning follows a sequence, generally moving from simple to more complex knowledge and skills. Finally, we chose the term *indicators* to emphasize that educators need evidence that children are developing the knowledge, skills, and understanding considered important for school and life readiness. To plan appropriately for students and to evaluate program effectiveness, we need observable indicators of our impact on children.

This book is designed to help you as you guide and support young children's learning in the Creative Arts content area in the HighScope Curriculum. This chapter provided insights from research literature on how children approach creative arts and summarized basic principles of how children acquire knowledge and skills in the arts. Chapter 2 describes general teaching strategies for Creative Arts and provides an overview of the KDIs for this content area.

Chapters 3–7, respectively, provide specific teaching strategies for each of the five KDIs in Creative Arts:

40. **Art:** Children express and represent what they observe, think, imagine, and feel through two- and three-dimensional art.
41. **Music:** Children express and represent what they observe, think, imagine, and feel through music.
42. **Movement:** Children express and represent what they observe, think, imagine, and feel through movement.
43. **Pretend play:** Children express and represent what they observe, think, imagine, and feel through pretend play.
44. **Appreciating the arts:** Children appreciate the creative arts.

At the end of each of these chapters is a chart showing ideas for scaffolding learning for that KDI. The chart will help you recognize the specific abilities that are developing at earlier, middle, and later stages of development and gives corresponding teaching strategies that adults can use to support and gently extend children's learning at each stage.

CHAPTER 2

General Teaching Strategies for Creative Arts

General Teaching Strategies

In order to realize the full potential that the creative arts provide, children need daily experiences with a wide range of artistic media and forms of self-expression. Moreover, these experiences need to occur in a supportive climate that accepts and values artistic experimentation, and does not pressure children to produce a "product" or stage a "performance" for the benefit of adults. To engage young children in the creative arts, and instill in them an early appreciation of their own and others' potential for artistic expression, use the general strategies described below as well as the specific ideas detailed under each Creative Arts key developmental indicator (KDI).

Provide open-ended art materials and experiences

As with all areas of early learning, young children thrive when they work with open-ended materials and explore actions and ideas that build on their own interests. This is nowhere more true than in the arts, where children explore drawing and modeling materials, listen and respond to different styles of music, represent actions and express emotions through movement, and imitate others and create new roles for themselves in pretend play. Remember too that many non-art materials help to develop the fine-motor, gross-motor, and eye-hand coordination skills that children can apply to their explorations in the creative arts. Having these basic perceptual and motor skills allows children to execute their artistic ideas with less frustration.

Because of the open-ended materials involved, the arts in particular allow children to explore actions and ideas that build on their own interests.

Choosing among forms of creative expression

Young children seem naturally drawn to one or more forms of creative expression. Many enjoy working with two- or three-dimensional art materials, whether sliding a paint-filled brush across the paper or squeezing wet clay between their hands. Children delight in singing songs and trying their hand at various percussion instruments. Inherently physical, preschoolers express their ideas and feelings through movement, sometimes experimenting with movement by itself and other times moving to the sounds of music. They readily use actions and props to imitate familiar roles or create pretend play scenarios for themselves and others. Providing a wide variety of materials that children can use and transform to suit their own purposes supports their artistic exploration and creative play. The materials listed in chapter 6 of *The HighScope Preschool Curriculum* (Epstein & Hohmann, 2012) for the art area, block area, house area, and movement and music area are especially suited for open-ended activities in the arts. Materials recommended for other areas, such as the sand and water table, toy area, and outdoor play space also lend themselves to artistic exploration. In fact, almost anything works in service of the arts!

Connecting art materials to children's lives

Educational consultants Walter Drew and Baji Rankin emphasize that open-ended materials and experiences allow children to connect the arts to their own lives. These connections make art meaningful and lead to more authentic artistic expression and genuine creativity. As children sort, manipulate, and discover the multiple possibilities of art materials, they act as scientists and engineers. "Key to this kind of work by children is the teacher's respect for both the child and the materials and the availability of open-ended materials like clay, paint, and the tools for drawing and writing. Materials can be reusable resources—quality, unwanted, manufacturing business by-products, otherwise destined for the landfill, which can serve as much-needed, open-ended resources: cloth remnants, foam, wire, leather, rubber, and wood. Open-ended materials are particularly effective because they have no predetermined use" (Drew & Rankin, 2005, p. 35).

Intentionally engaging children with art materials

Providing interesting and diverse materials is not enough to promote the development of artistic knowledge and skills, however. Adults need to be intentional about engaging children with these materials and tools and to plan group-time activities that help children discover and reflect on the cognitive and social possibilities embodied within the creative arts. "Adults must value the lessons to be learned from art and make a conscious decision to feature an arts program in the curriculum. Without this commitment from administrators and teachers, young children's artistic development will not extend beyond the conventional and unsophisticated. Attitudes as well as behavior will be affected; children will have lost an early opportunity to view art as a legitimate field of study. As a result, art educators agree that the intention to teach and respect art is vital to creating a climate in which art learning can thrive" (Epstein, 2007, p. 110).

Of course, this does not mean that teachers should be "directive" about how young children paint and sculpt, sing and chant, move their bodies, or carry out various roles in their pretend play. There is no research evidence that forcing children to copy a drawing, or perform any other artistic act in a prescribed manner, generalizes beyond the immediate task or leads to more mature artistic ability. In most cases, efforts to

These children explore their own ideas to discover how their bodies can move.

force specific representations lead to frustration for both adults and children. Even if there is temporary success — children may copy more details or make an approximate facsimile of the teacher's precut jack-o-lantern — the behavior will not carry over to the next artistic endeavor. Nor will it teach children anything meaningful about that art form. Moreover, it deprives children of discovering what the materials — and their own creative imaginations — can do.

Establish a climate that supports creative risk-taking and emphasizes process over product

Creating and appreciating the arts depends on having the freedom to explore and the confidence to take emotional risks. Children's artistic creativity thrives when they feel supported and know they will not be judged for what they do and say. Treat their attempts to create something or voice an artistic opinion as learning experiences, never as failures. Don't praise work as being "pretty" or second-guess children's artistic opinions. Children may play it "safe" in search of rewards or refrain from expressing their views if they fear correction, disagreement, or ridicule.

In *The Colors of Learning*, art educators Rosemary Althouse, Margaret Johnson, and Sharon Mitchell say "the atmosphere must be one in which the child thinks, 'It is all right for me to make a mistake. It is all right for me to choose this color. It is all right for me to mix these colors together to find out what color I can make'" (2003, p. 22). They emphasize that children are discouraged from using their imagination and creativity when teachers tell them what materials to use or require them to copy particular objects. Instead of directing children's artwork, accept what children make, and encourage them to describe the ideas behind it — "Tell me about all the colored dots in this corner"; "How did you move differently when the music got faster?" This not only helps children feel secure in their artistic expression, it also encourages the development of their critical thinking skills (Bodrova & Leong, 2007).

To establish a climate that supports artistic exploration, emphasize children's overall efforts rather than specific results. Focus on the process instead of the product. Allow ample time for experimentation, repetition, and reflection. Children develop depth in the arts only after they work with the same materials over and over again, discovering their properties and honing their expertise in using them. By letting children freely explore, they can eventually produce original and unique artistic works. Cutting this process short can actually stunt the flowering of their creativity.

Supporting process over product

Unfortunately, "the use of art materials to complete designs prepared and distributed by teachers is all but universal in the preschools and primary grades" (Thompson, 1995, p. 2). Even well-intentioned teachers often fall into the trap of having young children make "cute" things to satisfy an adult audience. You may need to gently explain to parents and school administrators why the demand to create a product is actually counterproductive to children's artistic development. Resist pressures to showcase "polished" artwork in school hallways or send home to be affixed to family refrigerators. Don't entice preschoolers to play "rehearsed" roles during performances staged for adults' amusement. Instead, point out what children learn when they explore materials, sing, move, and act out scenarios designed to satisfy only themselves and their own curiosity.

Encouraging collaboration

Another way to establish a supportive artistic climate is to encourage collaboration. Sometimes

Encouraging Creativity in Children

In *The Creative Spirit*, authors Daniel Goleman, Paul Kaufman, and Michael Ray (1993) identify seven ways that adults, often with good intentions, inadvertently discourage children's creativity. These are each summarized below, along with the counteracting strategies used in the HighScope Curriculum to encourage creative exploration and meaningful learning.

- ***Surveillance:*** Hovering over children and constantly watching them while they work can suppress their willingness to take creative risks.
  Instead: Give children time and space to work on their own. Be available for support but be sensitive to when children do not want your presence or interruption.
- ***Evaluation:*** When children worry about how adults perceive what they are doing, they cannot experience satisfaction with their own accomplishments.
  Instead: Accept whatever children create in their artistic exploration. Show interest, not judgment. Encourage them to describe their work in their own terms.
- ***Rewards:*** Using prizes deprives children of the intrinsic pleasure of creative activity.
  Instead: Let art be its own reward. Share their satisfaction with the creative process.

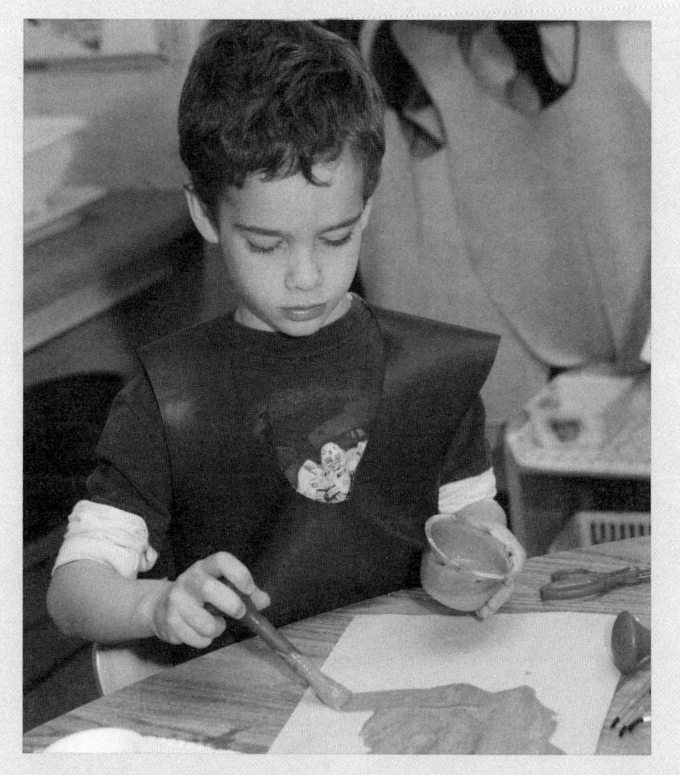

- ***Competition:*** Putting children in win-lose situations, where only one person can come out on top, does not let children progress at their own pace.
  Instead: Avoid competition. Value each child's creative activity for its own sake. Every child who wants should have his or her work displayed and have the chance to be the leader.
- ***Over-control:*** Telling children how to do things leaves them feeling as though their originality is a mistake. Exploration seems like a waste of time if adults are going to direct things anyway.
  Instead: Give children artistic freedom. Remember that encouraging their initiative leads to in-depth exploration and results in more meaningful learning in the long run.
- ***Restricting choice:*** When children are told what activities to do instead of following their own curiosity and passion, the experimentation that leads to creative discovery is further restricted.
  Instead: Give children authentic choices as they discover and explore the arts. They are more likely to engage with a variety of media and tools when they pursue their own interests.
- ***Pressure:*** Imposing expectations for performance, especially when they are beyond a child's developmental capabilities, can instill avoidance or dislike for a subject or activity.

  Instead: Emphasize process over product. Encourage children to pursue the creative arts for their own learning and satisfaction, not to meet the expectations of adults.

As these children bring their individual interpretation to a collaborative art project, they develop social skills and an artistic sensibility.

teachers are reluctant to have children work together because they are afraid of children "copying" — the opposite of individual creativity. However, children inevitably give their individual interpretation to any form of artistic expression. Moreover, collaboration makes children more observant of artistic elements and details in their own work. For example, Taunton and Colbert (2000) found that when children worked together during an art activity, they shared their observations about what they were drawing and how they chose to use the materials. This made children more reflective about the details of their own work, and they built on the ideas shared by their peers.

Thus, rather than limiting originality, observing and building on what other children and artists do actually spurs creative innovation. Ask children to share their explorations, discoveries, and aesthetic preferences with one another. The act of sharing engenders confidence because children have reason to think, "My ideas are worthwhile." Collaboration also builds trust when others accept and are interested in what each child contributes to the artistic endeavor. Children who are just learning about the creative arts may not always express themselves clearly, so be available to help explain and interpret their actions and ideas to one another when necessary (e.g., "Colin says he chose the yellow paint because it's bright like the sun"; "Brynna is asking you to pour in more water to make the dough squishier. She wants to squeeze it through her fingers").

Encourage children to represent real and imaginary experiences through the arts

Young children represent familiar objects, people, places, and events through all forms of artistic media. They make drawings, imitate sounds and movements, and create pretend play scenarios that depict family roles and interactions, the antics of pets, fears about going to the doctor, the anticipation of going to kindergarten, the ideal birthday party, and so on. They also use the arts to represent things that arise in their own or others' imaginations, such as scary monsters, storybook characters, magic kingdoms, or a concoction made by combining all their favorite foods.

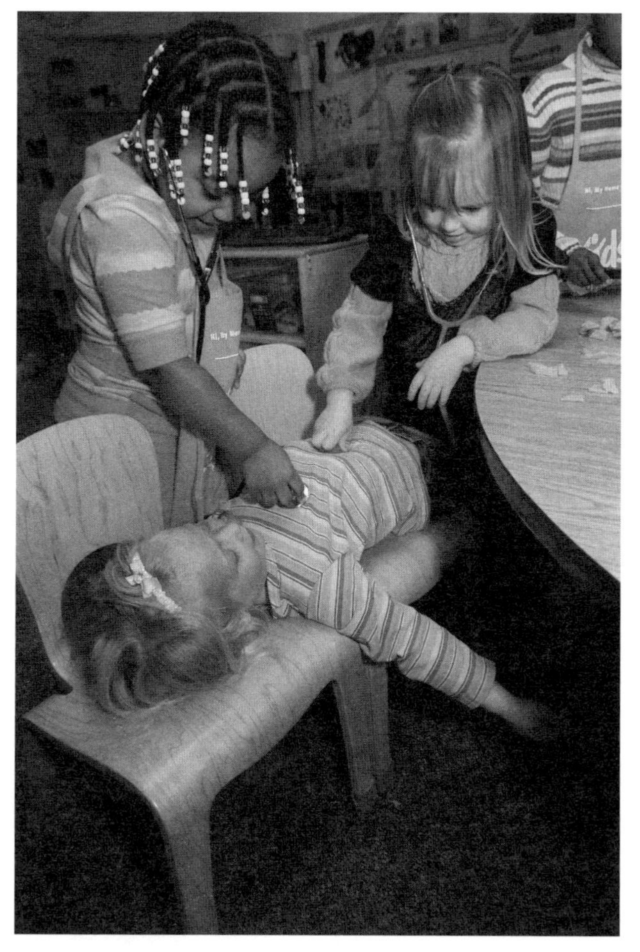

These children dramatize a visit to the doctor in their pretend play.

Scaffolding strategies

Although children seem to naturally create art from these real and imaginary circumstances, their play and use of materials can be quite stereotyped and unvarying without adult support to extend it (Kindler, 1995). You do not want to be directive by "telling" children what to draw or sing, how to move, or what roles to reenact. However, you can use appropriate scaffolding strategies to help them expand their choice and manipulation of materials, and to consider more options of how, what, when, where, and even why they represent their ideas and feelings. For example:

- At small-group time, reread a favorite book and suggest children use the art materials you provide to create their own stories or ideas. Children may represent a character or scene from the story, represent their own ideas, or just explore the materials. You have provided them with the opportunity to capture something meaningful to them through art.
- At large-group time, provide opportunities for children to re-create familiar and imaginary movements. For example, they might pretend to walk like big monsters with long legs or tiny insects with short legs. Likewise, you can play different types of music and encourage children to move like various animals, depending on the loudness or tempo of the music. Encourage children to label what they are imitating and to describe their movements.
- Take advantage of experiences that occur throughout the daily routine and ask children how they could draw, build, sing, move, or otherwise represent the people, materials, and events. Children might draw their plans, show what their hands were doing, or fill in the words to a familiar song to describe their

work-time activities at recall. Preschoolers can also represent field trips or other special events through the use of various artistic media. During transitions, encourage them to move like a "sleepy child" or cross the room as if they were riding a tricycle. Encourage children to suggest their own ideas for using the arts to represent daily actions and to describe and demonstrate them for others to copy or vary.

- Take photographs of the children engaged in various activities in the classroom and outside. Look at them together and talk about what is depicted. Talk with children about visual details and the sounds or movements that went along with the activity. During group times, provide materials to represent that activity or event in various ways, for example, by drawing or molding the people or materials, making up a rhyme or chant, moving their bodies, or reenacting their own and other people's roles. Encourage children to refer to the photos often so they can recall and incorporate more details in their creative representations.

Talk with children about the arts

The language of art contains words that preschoolers typically learn and use in other contexts. For example, early education focuses on terms related to color, shape, line, and size — what Smith et al. (1993) refer to as "visual-graphic elements." Many words used to describe and

As children become familiar with the language of the arts, encourage them to use these terms as they talk about their creations.

compare speech or physical activity, such as *louder* and *softer*, or *faster* and *slower*, apply equally well to music and movement activities. As children become familiar with this language in their other play and work, encourage them to also use these terms when they talk about the arts.

Fostering conversations

To elicit genuine conversations, encourage children to tell you about the art, music, movement, or pretend play scenarios they invent in their own words. Never presume to know what they have created, not only because you may be wrong, but also because you will deprive them of the chance to reflect on and describe their thoughts and actions themselves. Do the same when you ask children their opinions about art. Don't assume you know what they like and dislike, or what they find interesting about an image, sound, or movement. Be prepared to be surprised!

At work time in the art area, Miss Lucy says to Martin, "You drew a big circle with a smaller one inside it." Martin responds, "That's our fish tank and the new baby fish. There were more but the big fish ate them all up."

❖

"[The teacher] said to Maria, 'I see a dog in your picture.' Maria answered in a frustrated tone, 'That's not a dog; that's my mama.' Realizing his mistake, Mr. Allen responded, 'Tell me more about your mother.' This gave the child the opportunity to give more details about the picture" (Althouse et al., 2003, p. 55).

While too many comments or questions can end rather than extend a conversation, a well-timed remark or inquiry can lead to a mutually satisfying exchange between an adult and a child. Thoughtful statements, and divergent or open-ended questions can elicit thinking on the part of children and stimulate real discussions. Don't impose your ideas, but feel free to share them as long as children understand you are open to hearing their experiences and thoughts as well. For suggestions on language to support authentic dialogue with children about the arts, see "Encouraging Children to Talk About the Creative Arts" on pages 22–23.

Draw on the artistic forms in the cultures of children's families and communities

Before they arrive at preschool, young children have encountered the arts at home, in their local community, and in the broader culture. They may have been consciously introduced to the arts by their parents, for example, taken to children's museums or concerts. But even when this is not the case, children are inadvertently exposed to the culture's artistic tastes through images on posters, music playing in the environment, and characters depicted in publications and broadcast media. To deepen this exposure, especially in ways that support children's diverse cultural identities and affiliations, you can deliberately include representative artwork from every medium in the everyday furnishings, materials, and activities that make up the preschool setting.

The National Association for the Education of Young Children (NAEYC) regards broad exposure to the arts as an important social and cognitive component of the early childhood curriculum. "Teachers can use a variety of strategies to increase young children's awareness and appreciation of the arts in their own cultural and local communities and beyond. These include bringing the arts into the classroom (e.g., displaying prints of fine arts and books that include art reproductions); inviting community artists to

Encouraging Children to Talk About the Creative Arts

Thoughtful comments and occasional open-ended questions in which adults invite children's ideas can lead to genuine discussions about making and appreciating art. Here are some conversation openers that encourage children to share and reflect on their art experiences.

How does the _____ (material) feel (smell, sound, or other appropriate sense)?

For example, "How do the beads feel?" or "How does the clay smell?" or "How does the tambourine sound?"

What does the (sound, image) remind you of?

For example, "What does this slow music make you think of?" or "I wonder if this jagged shape reminds you of anything on the playground?"

How can we move to this (sound or music)?

For example, "Here's a quiet and slow song. How could we move to it?"

This _____ (image, sound, movement) makes me think of _____.

For example, "This dark red reminds me of the lipstick your mommy wears" or "That noise sounds like the fire truck that just went by."

I'm curious about how you made that. What did you use?

For example, "How did you build the boat?" or "Tell me what you used to make your boat."

How will you be the _____ (pretend role)? What will you use?

For example, "You're going to be the guy who puts out the fires. I wonder what you will use to do that."

How did you use the _____ (material or tool)?

For example, "I wonder how you used the chisel to make your bookends" or "I wonder how you made your scarves fly to the windy music?"

Tell us what you found out about the _____ (material or tool).

For example, "Jason used the tapestry hook today. Jason, what did you learn about using the tapestry hook?"

How did you do that _____ (movement)?

For example, "Show (tell) us how you jumped so we can all try to do it that way."

What did you do so the _____ (material or action) looks like _____ (describe effect)?

For example, "What did you do to make the paint so thick in this corner?" or "What did you do to make your arms spin around?"

Tell me/us/another child about the _____ (materials) you used or _____ (action) you did.

For example, "Liza, Alicia wants to know how you painted your cup yesterday so she can paint her bowl today" or "Max, how can I slide slowly from the chair to the door like you just did?"

What made you think of making/doing that?

For example, "Chris, what made you decide to make a doghouse?" or "Elena and Cherise, I wonder why you decided to both be the mommies."

What are some other ways to (use the material or tool) or (move to that sound)?

For example, "I wonder how else we can fold the paper" or "Let's see how else we can move to this bouncy music."

What do you think would happen if _____ (suggest a way to manipulate a material or move in a unique way)?

For example, "What do you suppose would happen if we dipped the yarn in water first?" or "What would happen if we didn't use our hands to move the balloons?"

I wonder how you could get the _____(material or your body) to _____ (act or move a certain way).

For example, "I wonder how you could get the paper to stand up?"or "How do you think you could make your arms go high and then low?"

I'd like to hear more about _____ (material, tool, or action).

For example, "I'd like to hear more about the way you used these brushes on the wood" or "Tell me more about the rules you made up for your speedboat race."

I wonder what's the same (or different) about these _____ (materials, sounds, or actions).

For example, "I wonder what's the same about the watercolor and tempera paints" or "What's different about these two notes?" or "Garth stretched his arms this way (demonstrate) and Keira stretched hers this way (demonstrate). How do you think they're the same? Different?"

These (images, sounds, actions) look (sound) different. I wonder why.

For example, "I wonder why your pictures look so different even though you both used blue paper and red markers" or "We all moved differently to the same fast music. I wonder why."

Why do you suppose the artist (painter, composer, dancer) made/did it that way?

For example, "I wonder why this artist paints big pictures and this one makes small pictures?" or "The first composer wrote fast notes and the second one wrote slow notes. Why do you suppose they each wrote their music a different way?"

Creative Arts in Action

KDI 40. Art

KDI 41. Music

KDI 42. Movement

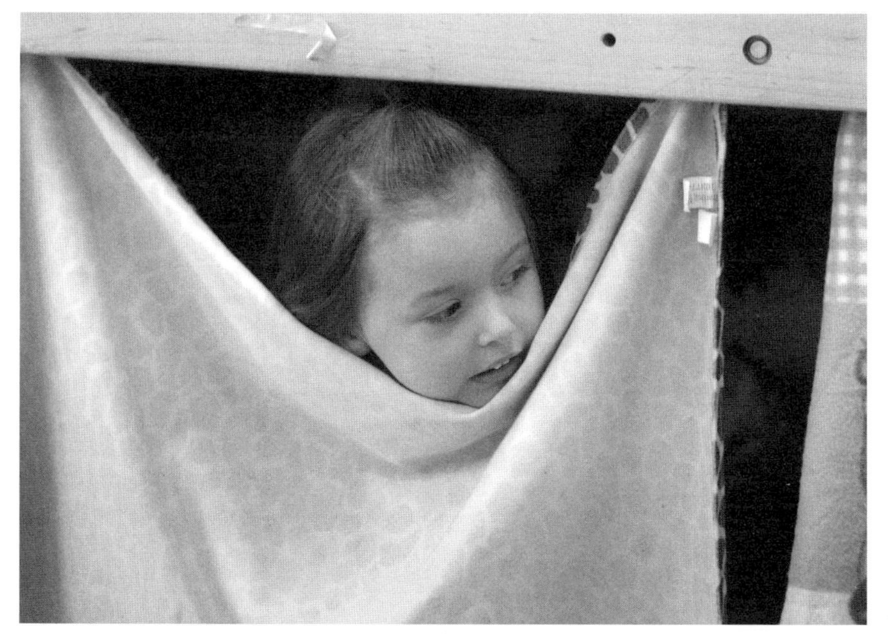

KDI 43. Pretend play

KDI 44. Appreciating the arts

Key Developmental Indicators in Creative Arts

F. Creative Arts

40. Art: Children express and represent what they observe, think, imagine, and feel through two- and three-dimensional art.
Description: Children explore and use a variety of materials and tools to draw and paint, mold and sculpt, build and assemble. They use the properties of art materials (e.g., shape, color, texture) to represent their ideas. Children's representations and designs develop from simple to complex and from accidental to intentional.

41. Music: Children express and represent what they observe, think, imagine, and feel through music.
Description: Children explore and experience sound through singing, moving, listening, and playing instruments. They experiment with their voices and make up songs and chants. Children explore and respond to musical elements such as pitch (high, low), tempo (fast, slow), dynamics (loud, soft), and steady beat.

42. Movement: Children express and represent what they observe, think, imagine, and feel through movement.
Description: Children explore moving their whole bodies, or parts of their bodies, with and without music. They respond to the features and moods of music through movement.

43. Pretend play: Children express and represent what they observe, think, imagine, and feel through pretend play.
Description: Children imitate actions, use one object to stand for another, and take on roles themselves based on their interests and experiences. They use figures to represent characters in their pretend scenarios (e.g., having a "family" of toy bears talk to one another). Their play themes develop in detail and complexity over time.

44. Appreciating the arts: Children appreciate the creative arts.
Description: Children express opinions and preferences about the arts. They identify the pieces (e.g., a painting or musical selection) and styles they do or do not like and offer simple explanations about why. Children describe the effects they and other artists create and develop a vocabulary to talk about the arts.

visit or going to their studios; and taking field trips to galleries, museums, performances, and public art displays" (Copple & Bredekamp, 2009, p. 176). While the arts play a special role at holiday times, don't overlook their presence in families' everyday lives. Just as you incorporate things such as food, clothing, and family roles, as well as celebrations, to enhance children's self-identity and appreciation for diversity, think of how the arts can also contribute to these areas of development.

Contact local arts groups and libraries to find out what resources are specifically available for young children, and work with staff at these organizations to make sure they know the interests and developmental levels of your children. Many communities have programs and grants to welcome children into museums, artists' studios, and performance spaces, as well as to bring the arts and artists directly to children in their educational settings. You needn't be in a large urban setting to find and take advantage of these offerings. Research the options in your area.

Remember that families are also a resource. Encourage them to share their artistic interests and talents. For example, perhaps a parent weaves or takes photographs, plays an instrument, belongs to a folk dance group, sings in a choir, or performs with a community theater group. Invite them to share these interests with the class — in a small or large group, during work time, or on a field trip. Work with them to ensure the session will be hands-on and appropriate for all the children who participate. Families may be willing to loan artwork to the class, such as a carving or wall hanging, for a period of time, especially something they see as representative of their culture. Encourage children to talk about where these things are displayed and used in their own homes. Include different genres and styles that children experience at home in movement and music activities.

Key Developmental Indicators

HighScope has five **key developmental indicators (KDIs)** in creative arts: 40. Art, 41. Music, 42. Movement, 43. Pretend play, and 44. Appreciating the arts.

Chapters 3–7 discuss the knowledge and skills young children acquire in each of these KDIs and the specific teaching strategies adults can use to support artistic development in young children. At the end of each chapter is a "scaffolding chart" with examples of what children might say and do at early, middle, and later stages of creative development, and how adults can scaffold their learning through appropriate support and gentle extensions. These charts offer additional ideas on how you might carry out the strategies in the following chapters during play and other interactions with children.

CHAPTER 3

KDI 40. Art

F. Creative Arts

40. Art: Children express and represent what they observe, think, imagine, and feel through two- and three-dimensional art.

Description: Children explore and use a variety of materials and tools to draw and paint, mold and sculpt, build and assemble. They use the properties of art materials (e.g., shape, color, texture) to represent their ideas. Children's representations and designs develop from simple to complex and from accidental to intentional.

At outside time, Carol makes squiggle lines with a stick in the dirt. Marco draws circles with his stick, while Flora draws a checkerboard and then uses the point of her stick to poke a hole in the middle of each square.

❖

At work time in the art area, Tanya staples feathers to a paper crown and says, "Look, it has polka dots."

❖

At work time in the toy area, David uses Magna-Tiles to make an airport with a runway, a "plane house," and a plane. He flies the plane around the airport and lands on the runway.

❖

At work time in the art area, Jayla says she wants to make a "parade." (She and her family had gone to a July 4th parade that weekend.) She puts beads in a cup, covers the cup with foil and tape, then shakes it and says it's a "maraca."

Children's interest in making art appears to be universal (Thompson, 1995). In addition to using standard art materials furnished by adults, children the world over draw in the sand, mold with mud, scratch with stones on pavement, interlace yarn, and otherwise work with whatever is at hand. This drive to create visual art stems from multiple sources during the preschool years. One factor is the simple joy young children derive from exploring materials and tools. Another is their emerging ability to represent what they see and feel using visual images. Additionally, as their sense of self develops, children may have the desire to literally leave their mark on the world.

How Art Develops

The role of visual art in the early childhood curriculum

Given the young child's inherent motivation to create visual art, it is not surprising that educators regard making art as a standard component of the early childhood curriculum. Florence Goodenough, one of the earliest art theorists, emphasized that "to little children, drawing is a language—a form of cognitive expression—and its purpose is not primarily esthetic" (1926, p. 14). Friedrich Froebel saw the arts as a kind of pre-occupational training, and children in the first kindergarten programs wove place mats, punched designs in paper, and folded paper to create ornate shapes (Seefeldt, 1999). Advocates of the early nursery school movement, however, believed art should foster children's freedom of expression and emphasized using raw materials such as clay, paint, and crayons (Beatty, 1995). Rather than urging children to make specific products, they believed in giving them free reign to express their creative visions and inner emotions, and enjoy the uninhibited use of artistic media.

At small-group time, Royce uses markers to draw three figures that he labels "giant, superhero, and Rachel" (his teacher). Each has a head with eyes and a mouth, and very long legs. "Now they can run away really fast when the monster tries to get them," he tells Rachel.

The importance of artistic expression in early development and education was further supported from the 1950s through the 1970s by the work of theorists such as Viktor Lowenfeld (1947). It gained additional adherents in the 1980s and 1990s when visual art was one of the "multiple intelligences" recognized by Howard Gardner (1982) and his colleagues at Project Zero. While an emphasis on academics has weakened time and funding for arts education in the last decade, there is a renewed interest in the potential of art to close the achievement gap by engaging the enthusiasm of children who are at risk of school failure (Fiske, 1999). In addition to educators, business leaders increasingly view the arts as vital to developing children's critical thinking skills and helping the country maintain its global competitive edge (Americans for the Arts, 2010).

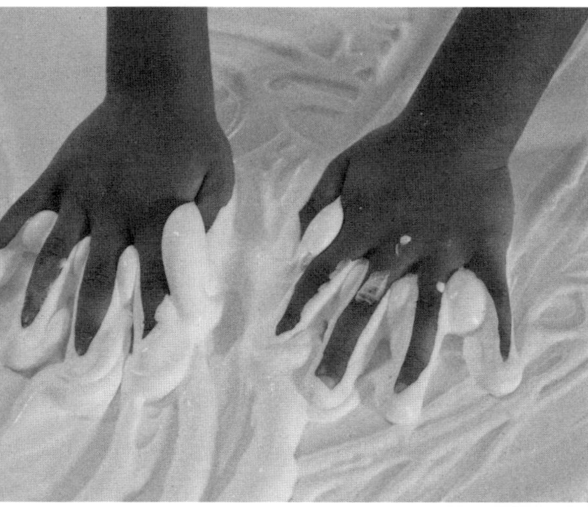

Factors affecting early art development

Changes in young children's cognitive, social-emotional, perceptual, and physical growth are all reflected in their visual art. As noted above, the cognitive ability to hold mental images in mind and then represent them in two and three dimensions allows preschoolers to engage in the symbolic aspects of art. Young children are also able to express their feelings through various visual media, and to take perspectives outside their own as they consider the artwork made by others. A growing awareness of and ability to label the properties of objects (their color, size, and shape) not only makes preschoolers more observant, but allows them to make conscious choices about how they re-create what they see. Finally, increasing motor control and eye-hand coordination permits them to use materials and tools with growing skill as they translate mental images into concrete representations.

At work time in the art area, Brianna holds up "barbells" she has made by attaching two play dough balls to the end of a paper towel tube and says, "Look at my muscles."

❖

At work time in the block area, Donna hammers three pieces of wood together to make an airplane: a long piece for the body, a medium piece for the wings, and a short one for the tail.

❖

At work time in the book area, Ben makes a "boy puppet" by stapling paper strips for arms and legs to a head and body made from a piece of cardboard with a slit in the middle.

Stages of art development

Art theorists have long attempted to describe the stages of artistic development in children. This endeavor is complicated by the fact that artistic behavior is affected not only by maturation, but also by cultural factors, instruction from adults, and innate talent (Seefeldt, 1999). For example, preferences for representing the human form vary by culture. (Drawing people is less acceptable in Islamic societies.) Even limited adult assistance can affect the level of complexity in children's art. Simply encouraging children to focus on specific details when they observe something (such as the facial features of another person) results in more detail in their visual representations. Studies of well-known artists, for example, confirm that attention to detail emerges early in their developmental history and continues throughout their artistic lives (Praisner, 1984).

Despite these legitimate debates and reservations about stage theory, there does seem to be a general progression within western cultures in children's visual art. Based on observations of children between the ages of one and seven years, Wolf and Perry (1989) documented a series of steps that begins with treating art materials as no different from other objects, to exploring the actions and properties of art materials, to naming "scribbles" and other visual representations, to trying to capture (represent) the basic features of objects, to striving for greater representational accuracy. (For more on artistic development in young children, see "Stages in Making and Appreciating Art" on p. 6.) Bearing this overall progression in mind, supportive adults should nevertheless scaffold each child's individual journey on the path to creative visual expression.

At small-group time, Douglas moves bobby pins around on the table. At one point, he arranges them in a circle. "Look," he says, delighted with his discovery, "It's a spider!"

❖

At work time in the block area, Trey announces he is making a drum set and tapes together three oatmeal boxes.

❖

At work time in the toy area, Corey molds play dough into a bumpy oblong, puts a small wooden bead on top of it, and then puts two small Tinkertoy sticks on either side of the bead. Using his deepest voice to make the sound of an engine, Corey "flies" it over the table.

Teaching Strategies That Support Art

Letting children express themselves freely through art is not the same thing as teachers adopting a "hands-off" attitude. On the contrary, adults need to actively and intentionally encourage children's artistic exploration for them to reap the maximum benefits of an art-rich environment. Therefore, in addition to the general strategies described above, use the following techniques to promote children's exploration and use of two- and three-dimensional art materials and tools.

Provide diverse examples of visual art throughout the learning environment

Children become aware of the role of visual art in their lives when they are surrounded by it. Adults typically think of art as a painting hanging on the wall or a sculpture sitting on a pedestal. However, art is also present in many everyday objects, for example, the colorful design of a sweater, the shape and patterning of a hand-carved salad bowl, the graceful curves of a glass vase, the smooth texture of a porcelain plate, the scenic background in a family vacation photo, or the molded metal hinge on a wooden box. Nature also abounds in artistic elements such as color, shape, light and shadow, pattern, and texture. The more you encourage children to attend to the details in these kinds of objects and elements, the more they will use their hands and the materials available to convey the images imprinted on their minds.

Maddy divides a large square into four quadrants and fills each with a bright mix of colors and shapes. "It's like my grandma's crazy quilt," she says. "I helped her cut up the pieces."

❖

At outside time, Wyclef sorts fallen leaves into piles by color. "Red are my favorite," he says, and asks his teacher Jonathan to help him look for more. As they survey the yard, Wyclef notices lots of red leaves under one tree in particular. Jonathan tells him it's a maple tree. When his father comes to pick him up, Wyclef asks if they have a maple tree in their yard.

❖

At work time in the book area, Naomi and Marianna sit side by side and turn the pages of a wallpaper sample book. When they get to a page with small blue and lavender flowers, Naomi says, "My mommy has a sun dress like that, only her flowers are pink."

To ensure that children understand the role of art in human experience, provide diverse examples throughout the classroom and call attention to art in nature. For example, when you choose items for the house area, include colorful bowls, patterned baskets, and dress-up clothes made of interesting fabrics with eye-catching accessories. Ask families to donate decorative items from home that they no longer use. Select books whose illustrations represent

These children work in an art area with plentiful materials and different examples of art on the walls.

a wide range of artistic styles, including collage, realistic images, abstraction, black-and-white line drawings, intense colors and soft pastels, and photographs. Provide magazines and catalogs that show different home furnishings, architectural styles, fashions, and travel scenes with a range of lighting and landscapes. Choose wooden blocks that are not only sturdy but that have interesting grain in the wood. Offer colorful scarves for children to move with at large-group time and call attention to the visual formations they make as children wave them in the air or let them blow in the wind. Now and then, take the time to arrange snacks artfully on a plate and discuss the patterns and textures with the children. Talk about the colors, patterns, and textures in the curtains or the upholstery on the couch. Almost any material or experience can be chosen or created with aesthetics in mind.

Daily encounters with diverse examples of art in the environment spurs children's imaginations. For example, when they see objects, people, and events depicted in book illustrations, children get the idea that they can use art to portray their own experiences and feelings. They begin to consider art as a daily factor in their own lives. Looking at the artwork of people from other eras and/or cultures can also serve as a concrete jumping off point for preschoolers, even if they have only a rudimentary idea of the time or place depicted. Just as someone else might be inspired to depict the deep orange of a setting sun or a lively horse pulling a carriage, so might children want to capture the swirls of a heavy snowstorm or the tray table they used on their first airplane trip.

Give children time to explore art materials and tools in depth

While providing children with open-ended materials is critical, it is not enough to help them develop knowledge and skills in art. They also need time to explore those materials in depth. "Children continually presented with new media are never able to gain control over, or develop skill in, the use of any one medium and may not be able to acquire the skills and techniques necessary to actually use these materials to create art" (Seefeldt, 1999, p. 209). Instead of being flooded with materials, young children need unpressured time to investigate each one in depth.

So, in addition to giving children freedom to explore and create according to their own desires, be careful not to impose a timetable for them to try new media. In addition, provide safe areas to protect unfinished projects and "work-in-progress" signs so children can signal their intentions to continue working with the same materials over time.

At small-group time, Abby paints by rolling a golf ball dipped in green paint across her paper. Ursula watches and imitates her, using purple paint. They each use one ball, and the same color paint, for the entire session. First Abby, then Ursula, tries moving the ball in a circle, twisting it, dabbing it on the paper, and rolling it when the paint is almost dry.

❖

At small-group time, Maxwell holds three crayons in his fist and draws round and round on the paper. When the dense colors have filled the page (and sometimes overlapped onto the table), he asks his teacher to write "bird nest" across the bottom.

❖

At work time in the art area, Kim Soon paints at the easel and says to her teacher, "Look, I made purple. I used white, red, and blue." For the rest of work time, she mixes those colors in different proportions and paints a circle on the paper each time she creates a new variation.

Introduce art materials slowly. For example, during a small-group time activity, begin with one primary color — red, blue, or yellow. Let children thoroughly explore that single color and how it changes when they add white or black to it. Then they can start mixing two colors to create new colors. The same process applies to the gradual introduction of tools. Children should begin by using just their hands and experiencing the medium with their senses: "Does the paint feel wet or dry when I smear it with my fingers?" "Is the clay hard or soft?" "How much strength does it take to tear paper?" After children have manually explored the materials you introduce during a small-group time activity, begin to offer them tools such as brushes of different widths, or utensils to make impressions in clay. Later you can periodically introduce new materials and/or reintroduce old ones for children to explore in new ways. (For more ideas on providing sustained and in-depth art experiences to young children, see Epstein & Trimis, 2002.)

When given this opportunity to explore art materials in depth, children sometimes amaze adults with their persistence. However, it should come as no surprise that children maintain their focus when a project builds on their own interests and meets their own goals.

At work time in the art area, Danielle says, "I miss my grandma. I want to make her a card with a heart and a rainbow." After folding the paper and drawing a heart on the front, she takes the crayons out of the basket and lays them in a row on the table. One by one, she uses each color to draw an arc in the rainbow. She announces with satisfaction, "I used them all!"

❖

At work time in the block area, Arnie declares, "I need to make a crown so I can be the king. It will have diamonds all around the top." He cuts a strip of paper, draws diamonds on it with a blue marker, and fills them in with a red marker. Then he staples the ends of the paper strip together to make a circle. Making the crown, rather than being king, is more important to him at this point. When work time ends, Arnie is not quite done coloring in the diamonds. He sets the crown on the shelf with a "work-in-progress" sign and says he will finish it tomorrow. "Then me and Richie can play football kings," he announces.

Another aspect of time is the leisure to "make a mess" as children investigate the possibilities of the materials you provide. Adults may tend to offer a limited selection of "neat" materials (such as crayons and play dough) because they are afraid of children dripping, spilling, staining, and sticking — typical outcomes that also require additional cleanup time. Likewise, to minimize the mess, adults may control the conditions under which children use materials, for example, under supervision at small-group time instead of freely at work or choice time. However, only by making a mess will children experience the very properties you want them to discover about the media they are working with. They can help clean up and put away the materials when they are finished, just like they would in any other work-time activity.

It is also important for children to be given ample time to experience unconventional as well as conventional materials. Teachers sometimes limit art supplies to the ones they themselves are familiar with. However, you need not be an artist or be conversant with a wide array of media to encourage children to explore their artistic possibilities. For example, children can explore tearing, molding, weaving, and

It is important to provide children with open-ended art materials and to allow them to explore those materials at their own pace.

Exploring Paper as an Art Material

"The children in one preschool class began the year experimenting with paper. They tried tearing, twisting, crumbling, rolling, and other manipulations. Then they used scissors and hole punches, finally glue and paint. Later in the year, the teacher introduced the class to yarn and fabric. Again the children began working with their hands, then using tools such as scissors, crimpers, and large tapestry needles. They looked at books on weaving and quilting. Finally, they experimented with dyeing. After a few weeks, the teacher brought out the paper again. Children were excited to see an old 'friend,' but now they applied the stitching and dyeing techniques they had used with fiber to paper. Some tore or cut strips and wove 'paper tapestries.' Others painted squares of paper and arranged them in 'paper quilts.'"

— Epstein (2007, p. 116)

other artistic processes using scrap paper. Many other recycled materials offer unlimited (and inexpensive) possibilities for creativity.

Preschoolers also benefit from occasionally working with high-quality art supplies, not just inexpensive or disposable ones. They enjoy working with adult-like materials and tools, and the sophistication of their artwork will reflect this opportunity. For example, when preschoolers were given fine-bristled paintbrushes (one-quarter- to one-half-inch wide) instead of the traditional one-inch tools, they included significantly more detail in their easel paintings. Studies also show children fill more space and incorporate more detail when they draw with crayons, which have finer points and whose marks are easier to control, than markers (Seefeldt, 1999).

At work time in the art area, Ella uses a wide brush to paint the outline of a head and a body with arms and legs. She chooses a thin brush to paint the eyes, nose, mouth, hair, and eyebrows. After some consideration, she chooses a medium-width brush to paint a headband.

Finally, have fun exploring art materials and techniques yourself. Art researcher Anna Kindler (1995) found that when adults simply work alongside children, the children use art materials for a longer time, use them in more varied ways, and talk spontaneously about what they are doing. Use the materials the same way as the children do, copying their techniques and trying out their ideas. These actions will show you value the children's creativity and will help guide your discussions with them.

Display and send home children's artwork

Create opportunities for children to share their artwork with others. For example, display their artwork on the wall and on shelves throughout the room. Keeping these at eye level guarantees children will notice them and increases the likelihood children will talk spontaneously about the intentions and ideas behind their creations. Taking dictation about their artwork can further spur children to converse about the artwork on display. Write the dictation on a sticky note rather than directly on the artwork to show you respect what the child has done. Another key developmental indicator (KDI) book that is also part of the HighScope Preschool Curriculum set, *Language, Literacy, and Communication* (Epstein, 2012), describes how writing is a form of representation that children use to share their experiences, thoughts, and feelings. Remember that drawing and painting are also a form of writing for young children.

> Preschoolers' efforts at representation show their thinking and the effort they put into trying to depict objects and people with marks on the page. Drawing, in particular, is a child's first step toward writing. They often can describe their own creations verbally in far greater complexity ('This is a cat and here are his whiskers, and this is his tail') than they are able to achieve in their drawings, which may consist of only simple shapes and lines. Listening to what they have to say about their artwork can give teachers insights into children's thoughts and feelings (Copple & Bredekamp (2009, p. 177).

In addition to displaying artwork in the classroom, send children's creations home with parents. Displaying and sharing artwork, regardless of its artistic content or skill level, conveys to the child that his or her creations are important. Sometimes parents pressure children and their teachers to produce "refrigerator-ready" artwork. Help them understand and appreciate the value of exploration rather than production at this age. Explain how children benefit intellectually, socially, emotionally, and physically — as well as creatively — by being free and

In an activity combining art with letters, this child learns the letters of her name.

What Children Do and Learn Through Art

When young children are actively engaged in the process of exploring and creating with art, they:

- *Learn about the properties of materials* — Children discover and experiment with artistic attributes such as color, shape, line, and texture.
- *Enlarge their vocabulary* — Children learn the names of artistic properties and actions. They use words to describe how artwork looks and makes them feel.
- *Practice fine-motor skills and eye-hand coordination* — Children become increasingly adept at using art materials and tools. Their physical control in manipulating materials grows.
- *Develop observational skills* — Children learn to notice the visual and textural dimensions of what they want to depict. They pay increasing attention to visual details.
- *Increase their representational abilities* — Children use art to convey the images, emotions, and ideas in their mind. Art facilitates their ability to meet this important cognitive challenge.
- *Develop problem-solving skills* — Children think critically about how to use art materials and tools to best represent their ideas. They consider how to change their approach when their choice or manipulation of materials does not match their mental image of it.
- *Develop persistence* — Children explore art materials in depth when the endeavor stems from their own interests. They demonstrate perseverance and commitment carrying out their ideas.
- *Discover another means of self-expression* — Children use art as a "language" to express ideas and emotions. Art encourages them to reflect on what and how they want to communicate.

unpressured as they explore the world of visual art.

To see how preschoolers explore and create with art materials at different stages of development, and how adults can scaffold their learning in this area, see "Ideas for Scaffolding KDI. 40 Art." Use the ideas suggested in the chart to support and gently extend children's learning as you play and interact with them throughout the program day.

Ideas for Scaffolding KDI 40. Art

Always support children at their current level and occasionally offer a gentle extension.

Earlier	Middle	Later
Children may • Explore the sensory properties of one or two materials (e.g., squish play dough; "The paint is cold"). • Use art and building materials in non-representational ways (e.g., stack blocks, smear finger paint, pound golf tees in Styrofoam). • Work with materials and tools without being concerned about representing something (e.g., scribble lines, mold clay into blobs).	*Children may* • Notice the effects created by materials or tools (e.g., using a wide brush, say "You can make fat worms with this brush"). • Make simple representations with one or two basic features (e.g., paint a circle with two dots for the eyes and a straight line for the mouth to represent a person; stack two blocks to represent a "tall house"). • Accidentally create an image and then recognize that it can represent something (e.g., roll clay into a log; say, "Hey! That looks like a snake").	*Children may* • Use the properties (e.g., shape, color, texture) of materials or tools to represent something or create an effect (e.g., use a garlic press to make play dough hair). • Make complex representations with several details (e.g., draw a person with a head, torso, legs, and arms; form a bowl with clay, fill it with balls as "berries," and insert a plastic spoon). • Intentionally represent something (e.g., say "I'm going to make a dog" and draw a circle with four legs, a tail, ears, and facial features).
To support children's current level, adults can • Work with materials alongside children. • Imitate children's actions with materials and tools. • Accept children's interest in exploring materials without trying to make something.	*To support children's current level, adults can* • Comment on the effects children create with materials and tools (e.g., "A wide brush does make a fat line"). • Comment on the features in children's artwork (e.g., "You made a circle and put dots around the outside of it"). • Acknowledge that an image looks like what the child says it is (e.g., "That is round like the sun!").	*To support children's current level, adults can* • Acknowledge when children create effects with materials and tools (e.g., "The garlic press makes the play dough look like hair"). • Talk about details children add to their artwork (e.g., "You mixed blue and green for the eyes. What about the hair?"). • Ask children what and how they will make something (e.g., "What will your dog look like? How will you make it?").
To offer a gentle extension, adults can • Gradually introduce new materials and tools. • Ask children to describe what they did so you can do the same thing (e.g., "Tell me how to make a mark just like yours"). • Label simple representations yourself (e.g., refer to a ball of clay as a "meatball").	*To offer a gentle extension, adults can* • Encourage children to anticipate the effects they create (e.g., "What do you think will happen with this brush?"). • Wonder what other details children could add (e.g., "I wonder what else you will add to your house"). • Model making and labeling something (e.g., say, "I'm going to make a spaceship and use these long pieces as the wings").	*To offer a gentle extension, adults can* • Provide art vocabulary words for what children create (e.g., "Adding white made the blue a lighter tint"). • Encourage children to look at real objects and perhaps add details (e.g., a mirror if they want to add more facial features). • Encourage children to represent their experiences (e.g., a field trip) at small-group time (accept if they choose not to).

KDI 41. Music

F. Creative Arts

41. Music: Children express and represent what they observe, think, imagine, and feel through music.

Description: Children explore and experience sound through singing, moving, listening, and playing instruments. They experiment with their voices and make up songs and chants. Children explore and respond to musical elements such as pitch (high, low), tempo (fast, slow), dynamics (loud, soft), and steady beat.

At large-group time, when it is his turn to pick a song, Todd turns to "Twinkle, Twinkle, Little Star" in the class songbook and immediately begins singing the words.

❖

At work time in the toy area, Wendy makes up a song about cows and sheep, in random pitches, as she plays with the farm animals.

❖

At work time in the toy area, Brianna makes up a song to the tune of "Row, Row, Row Your Boat" as she plays with the Lego horses. She sings, "Open, open, open the door. Let the horses go outside."

Young children and music are natural partners. Newborns respond to music by wriggling with pleasure or by being lulled to sleep, depending on the music's mood and tempo. Toddlers babble in musical tones, repeat song fragments, and create two- and three-note sequences. Preschoolers can differentiate musical styles and associate them with familiar situations ("That sounds like a parade!" "It's scary music!"). Young children also enjoy moving to music and playing simple instruments. Given their increased facility with language, three- and four-year-olds can learn entire songs, invent new words for familiar songs, and create their own simple melodies (often with random pitches) along with accompanying words. Like the other areas of the creative arts, music is a language that young children can use to communicate their thoughts and feelings.

How Music Develops

Developing musical knowledge and skill involves learning about rhythmic qualities (such as beat, rhythm, and tempo[2]) and tonal qualities (such as pitch and melody[3]). Research shows the child's intuitive aptitude — being able to think in rhythmic and tonal patterns — stabilizes at about age nine (Gordon, 1989). Young children also begin to develop ideas about music's emotional component, and spontaneously use and create music during their free play. Thus, "the early childhood years are critical to the development of the child's potential for comprehending and

[2]"Steady beat is the consistent, repetitive pulse that lies within every rhyme, song, or musical selection" and "rhythm is superimposed on the steady beat of a rhyme or song" (Weikart, 2000, pp. 123–124), i.e., in rhythm, the duration of sound can vary such that words may be sung or chanted quickly or slowly, with one or more syllables per beat. "Tempo is the speed at which musical sound progresses in time" (Stellaccio & McCarthy, 1999, p. 192), i.e., from slow to fast.

[3]"Pitch is the 'highness' or 'lowness' of a musical tone as determined by the number of vibrations per second" and "melody is an organized succession of pitches" (Stellaccio & McCarthy, 1999, pp. 191–192).

producing music," say music educators Cherie Stellaccio and Marie McCarthy (1999, p. 179).

Developing rhythmic knowledge

Perceiving the "time" elements of sound is fundamental to understanding and creating music. Perhaps that is why young children are generally able to perceive variations in beat (underlying pulse), rhythm (sound duration), and tempo (speed) before they develop concepts about pitch, melody, and harmony (Sims, 1991). While the ability to perceive and copy rhythmic regularity begins in toddlerhood, a sense of rhythmic structure is much better established in preschool (Stellaccio & McCarthy, 1999). Key to this development is having repeated experiences with music that has a prominent beat (Metz, 1989; Weikart, 2000).

At large-group time in the block area, Tasha taps drum sticks to the beat and hums along to music that her teacher puts on the CD player.

❖

At large-group time, the children shake tambourines to the beat of "Jingle Bells."

These children's ability to perceive rhythm, pattern, and change in music will help their learning in other areas, such as visual art, mathematics, and science.

The ability to hear, copy, and create the timing elements of music is related to other aspects of early perceptual and cognitive development (Hargreaves & Zimmerman, 1992). For example, general pattern awareness helps young children perceive musical regularities, while understanding concepts such as "change" and "more/less" attunes children to "faster/slower" variations in tempo. The ability to detect these basic musical elements in turn helps to facilitate learning in other areas, such as visual art (detecting visual patterns), mathematics (recognizing increasing and decreasing quantities), and science (understanding transformation and change).

Developing tonal knowledge

A great deal of research has been done on children's early vocal development (Stellaccio & McCarthy, 1999). Infants as young as 3–4 months experiment with sound, trying to match the pitch of their voice to a wide range of sounds. Toddlers can reproduce melodic intervals (match singing one note and then another higher or lower note). By age three, children can sing with a lyrical quality, and by age five tonal stability is well established. However, the ability to differentiate notes along a scale ("tonal competence") is highly dependent on children's early experience. Moreover, the experience must be active. For example, young children who sing and move their bodies high or low to match their singing voice have greater pitch awareness than those who just listen to the music (Scott-Kasner, 1992).

At outside time, Andrew pokes sticks in mud puddles and repeatedly sings, "Mud, mud, I love mud." He sings the first "mud" at a higher pitch and the second "mud" at a lower pitch.

❖

At work time in the house area, Jason pretends to be a puppy. "My voice is light and sweet," he says. Later in the same pretend play episode, he says, "My voice is getting lower and I'm getting older."

Understanding the emotional elements in music

Music also has emotional qualities. It is well established that music can have a powerful effect on our feelings. A musical experience has been likened to empathy, in that the listener responds to the emotions the composer wants to evoke. Music is thus a form of "social interaction" (Stellaccio & McCarthy, 1999). Children are also highly influenced by the emotional responses and musical preferences of their families and other significant people in their lives.

While these emotional factors seem self-evident, there is actually very little research on the development of affective responses to music, mostly because it is not an easy topic to study. Young children have limited vocabularies to describe their emotional reactions in general, and studies show it is easier for preschoolers to describe their feelings about visual and tactile stimuli than auditory ones (McMahon, 1987). Nevertheless, based on behavioral observations (such as when children request certain types of music or talk about how they will move to a particular piece of music), children do respond to the emotional components of different musical styles. They differentiate between music that engages them to participate in some way, such as lively music they can nod, pat, skip or bounce to versus slow or soft music that lends itself to quieting down and cuddling with a person, book, blanket, or toy.

Musical creativity and play

Young children reveal a natural inventiveness in chanting, singing, and instrumental experimentation during free play. Observations of children aged one through eight show they use their voices and instruments to compare pitches, copy and create simple melodies, experiment with timing, and express emotions (Moorhead & Pond, 1941/1978). Preschoolers spontaneously use vocalization and rhythmic movement to describe events, act out roles, or express feelings during play (Tarnowski & Leclerc, 1994). They inflect their voices to depict animals or machines (a rhythmic barking or steady hum), and make up or vary familiar songs to accompany their actions such as hammering or rocking a doll.

Children naturally express their feelings by moving to music.

At work time in the block area, Denny and Carlos say "Woo-woo-woo" as they drive their trains over the tracks they have built.

❖

At work time in the art area, after Ella and Emily (her teacher) finish washing their babies at the water table, Ella says, "Now we need to dry them off." As she gets a towel, she makes up and sings this song: "Dry, dry, dry the babies. Dry them nice and clean."

Not surprisingly, children in open-ended play settings engage in more of these spontaneous musical behaviors than those in highly adult-directed programs. This free exploration of music is critical to the development of children's vocal and rhythmic skills (Stellaccio & McCarthy, 1999). However, while it's true that children who are given the opportunity do engage in a great deal of musical exploration, that does not mean that music education should be left to chance.

Early childhood teachers need to be intentional about providing musical experiences in the same way they expose children to the other creative arts, and to academic and social learning in general. Though some educators may feel insecure about their role as music teachers, professors Kristen Kemple, Jacqueline Batey, and Lynn Hartle point out that "young children engage in music as play. Though many early childhood educators may not consider themselves musicians or music educators, they generally do feel comfortable with the medium of play" (2005, p. 25).

Learning about music is like any other exploratory activity that is "interactive, social, creative, and joyful" (Kemple et al., 2005, p. 25). Incorporating music throughout the program day allows preschoolers to discover its many qualities and use them to enhance their play and learning.

> Most young children are uninhibited, enthusiastic performers and lovers of music and movement, both of which enrich children's lives and learning in many ways. These should be a focused part of the day and also be integrated with other content areas. For example, music can help children learn phonological awareness, patterns, and counting. In addition, music helps English language learners learn new words and brings their cultures into the classroom (Copple & Bredekamp (2009, p. 177).

Children's spontaneous music play is especially enhanced when they hear and see adults singing in the classroom. Recorded music (such as CDs) is abstract because children cannot see the musicians and how they use their mouths to produce various sounds. Also, the tempo of most recordings is to too fast for young children to sing along. So, while recorded music is a useful tool (e.g., for adults to learn a song before they teach it to children or to accompany children's movement activities), young children benefit from hearing and joining in live singing. Also, by hearing teachers make up songs or new verses to familiar songs, children are more likely to think of themselves as singers and to make up songs as part of their own creative play.

Teaching Strategies That Support Music

As with the other creative arts, children's engagement with music should focus on exploration and discovery, not on production or performance. Preschoolers develop musical literacy when music receives attention on its own and is also integrated into other daily activities. To help children enjoy listening, responding to, and creating music, use the teaching strategies described in this chapter.

Look for opportunities to listen to, identify, and create sounds with children

Sounds, like images, are one way to represent objects and events (e.g., a siren signifies an emergency vehicle). As their ability to form mental images grows, preschoolers enjoy listening to and identifying what different sounds represent. Support this interest by calling their attention to the indoor and outdoor sounds that naturally occur around them, such as birdsong, wind, traffic, school bells, ticking clocks, doors opening and closing, rain on the roof, or a telephone ringing. In addition to these environmental sounds, provide noise-making materials, such as instruments, music players, timers, wind-up clocks, or computer programs that talk. Also include things children can use or combine to make their own sounds, such as beads or pebbles to shake in a pan, wooden sticks to bang together, sandpaper to rub on different types of surfaces, or water to squirt from a hose onto the pavement.

At greeting circle, Brian runs inside the classroom and excitedly tells his teacher, "Grandpa and me heard the mourning doves on our way to the car. They sounded like: Hoo, hoo, hoo!"

❖

At large-group time, Abby ties a shoelace to a flexible plastic "spider web" and twirls it over her head. "Listen," she says to her teacher. "Do you hear that sound?...It's the wind, but not the real wind, because that's outdoors." The teacher says to the other children, "I wonder if our voices can make that sound."

To help draw children's attention to sound, be intentional about creating opportunities to listen. For example, before going outside, you might say, "I wonder what we'll hear if we're

This teacher and a group of children experiment with making sounds through a cardboard tube.

quiet." Play sound guessing games at snack- or mealtimes. In addition to guessing frequently heard sounds (hammering in the woodworking area), include a few unusual or unfamiliar ones — such as dried beans being poured into a metal pan — to spark discussion and creative problem solving. As children listen and move to musical recordings at large-group times, occasionally comment on the sound of familiar instruments if they relate to the children's own actions and interests (e.g., "You're bouncing to the plinky sound of the piano"). Record sounds on a neighborhood walk and listen to and identify them with the children as you recall the experience together.

Encourage children to describe as well as label sounds. Comment if they do this spontaneously, and converse about the sounds children hear and make. Show interest in and accept the words they choose, and provide additional terms to expand children's vocabulary about sound.

One day when it rains too hard to go outside, the class gathers at the window. The teacher says, "Listen to the rain. How does it sound?" The words the children come up with include: drip-drop; like when mommy fills the bathtub; *and* my dog's toenails on the floor.

❖

At work time in the art area, Shelby whips paint in a bowl with an egg beater. She tells Tyrone, "It's my whizzle stick because it goes whizz."

❖

At small-group time, as Devon plays with a set of blocks, his teacher says, "You're banging the blocks together." Devon replies, "They're going click, clack, click, clack."

Children also enjoy creating sounds. For example, during pretend play, they often use their voices to act out roles ("Waaa, I'm a baby"), imitate the sounds of machines ("Crrrch" or "Jing-jing"), and call attention to their actions and discoveries ("Mmmm, yummy mud cakes!").

At snack time, while waiting for his food, Sylvan makes random vocal sounds that vary in pitch and length. He makes a long, high sound and says, "That's my apple juice noise."

❖

At work time, Terri plays with the dinosaur figures. She makes the sound of a large one by roaring in a low and loud tone, and the sound of a small one by making a high and soft sound.

Apart from enriching their pretend play, children simply enjoy exploring the range of sounds their voices can produce. You can support this interest by listening to and imitating their sounds, offering comments and acknowledgments, and encouraging children to try vocal variations.

At large-group time, when Mara waves a scarf over her head and says, "Whoosh," her teacher does the same. Several other children imitate the action and sound too.

❖

At outside time, Billy chants "Whee, I fell on my knee" while standing and falling in place. Then he runs in a circle, making exaggerated "whee" sounds, extending them longer and longer. His teacher echoes the sounds he makes, matching their pitch and length.

❖

At large-group time, the children respond to the teacher's ideas: "I wonder if we can make our voices go up really high." Felix stands on his toes "to make my voice higher." Katie says, "Now let's go really low," and the children make low sounds. Some get down on the ground.

Sing with children

Children like to sing and should have the opportunity to sing every day. They sing to hear and enjoy the sound of their own voices and the voices of other children and adults. You can create many opportunities for children to use their singing voices throughout the daily routine. Do not, however, play recorded music for children to sing along to. It is too distracting for them to try to listen and reproduce what they hear, and they may be discouraged when they cannot match it.

Young children enjoy singing many types of music including the sing-song of nursery rhymes ("Rain, Rain, Go Away" or "Baa, Baa, Black Sheep"), traditional children's songs ("The Farmer in the Dell" or "If You're Happy and You Know It"), simple folk songs ("She'll Be Comin' 'Round the Mountain" or "Are You Sleeping?"), and songs for special occasions ("Happy Birthday," "Jingle Bells," or "The Dreidl Song"). Gradually introduce and repeat these and other songs. Invite parents to begin and end parent meetings with a song they sing at home that you can teach to the children at school. By the end of the program year, you and the children can have quite a repertoire of songs that children can recognize and are able to sing.

Introducing a song

To introduce a new song, first establish a steady beat, for example, by patting it on your knees with both hands. Encourage children to pat the beat with you. Once the beat is established, sing the song through so the children can hear the melody and the words. The song's pitch should be on the high side because children's short vocal cords make it easier for them to sing in a higher range. Sing the entire song through several times. More children will start to join in as the melody and words become familiar, either humming along and/or singing the words they know. Repeat the song several days in a row to

Children love to sing! Look for opportunities for children to sing throughout the daily routine.

Singing Songs With Children

Use your voice, not a CD. When you are the musical source, you can adjust the tempo of the song to the task, the children's tempos, how high or low they can sing comfortably, or the ability level of your group. Recordings are abstract, and children cannot see the musicians or watch the mouth of the singer. Children will be encouraged to sing when they see and hear it modeled by you. Use the following tips when singing songs in your class:

- *Introducing new songs.* Children start a movement in steady beat. As the leader, synchronize the movement for the children by using a word for each movement (e.g., "Beat, beat, beat, listen" or "Pat, pat, pat, listen" or "March, march, march, listen"). Sing the song on a neutral syllable, such as "bah" or "la"... [which] provides the children the opportunity to listen to the melody. After repeating the melody using a neutral syllable several times, encourage the children to join in as they feel comfortable with the melody. Then, after they feel comfortable with the melody, have the children once again start a movement in steady beat. Synchronize the movement for the group by using an anchor word (e.g., "Beat, beat, beat, listen"). This time, sing the song with the words while the children keep the steady beat.
- *Learning all phrases of new songs.* Children start a movement in steady beat. Synchronize the movement for the children by adding the anchor pitch sung on the beginning pitch of the song (e.g., "Beat, beat, beat, sing"). Sing the first phrase of the song several times. Encourage the children to join in as they feel comfortable with the song. Use the same process, and sing the first and second phrases of the song several times. Use the same process to learn the third phrase and then the third and fourth phrases. Use the same process and sing the entire song several times as a class.
- *Singing familiar songs together.* Children start a movement in steady beat. Synchronize the movement for the children by adding the anchor pitch sung on the beginning pitch of the song (e.g., "Beat, beat, beat, and sing" or "One, two, sing with me"), and sing the song together.

— Haraksin-Probst, Hutson-Brandhagen, & Weikart (2008, p. 8)

enable more children to learn it. Return to familiar songs often as you gradually introduce new songs into the classroom repertoire.

Use singing in a variety of contexts. Large-group time is a natural time to sing and move to music (see KDI 42. Movement). Less experienced singers can easily join in with more practiced ones and have an opportunity to hone skills. You can also sing with children as they move between areas during transitions. Cleanup time is easier when accompanied by singing. For example, the song "This is the Way We..." can be adapted to sing about putting things away ("This is the way we wash the table" or "This is the way we stack the blocks").

At large-group time, when Henry chooses "Hickory Dickory Dock," Tai says, "The mouse ran up the clock." While the group sings the song, Frieda pats her hands on her legs to the beat.

❖

During the transition from planning to work time, Olivia sings, "I'm going to the house area" to the tune of "Did You Ever See a Lassie," a song the children often make up words to at large-group time.

❖

At cleanup time, when the teacher puts on the cleanup song, Corretta hums and spins as she carries blocks to the shelf.

Finding opportunities to sing

Be creative about finding other opportunities to sing during the day. For example, sing comments to heighten children's attention (sing "Five minutes 'til cleanup time") or describe something they've done (while sitting beside a child who is sorting blocks at work time, chant "Blue, blue, blue square here. Red square over there" to the tune of "Row, Row, Row Your Boat"). Children might enjoy "singing" their plans or singing along to a recall song that you made up to describe what they did at work time. Read books that illustrate familiar songs. Children can also make drawings or build models to represent and add their own details to familiar songs.

Initiate singing games at small- or large-group time. For example, sing a neutral syllable (such as *la*), hum, or play the first few notes of a familiar song for children to guess what it is. After a few rounds, children can take turns singing a syllable or humming songs for others to identify. It does not matter if their singing or guessing is accurate; the significance of the experience is for children to create and listen for melody. Record children singing and see if they can identify one another's voices. (Since our voices sound different to ourselves, they may not be able to recognize their own voices.) Another game is pitch-matching. Sing or play two notes and invite children to repeat them, listening to hear whether their voices should go higher or lower on the second note. Again, it does not matter if they match the pitches exactly. That will come with time and the experiences you provide for them to hear and practice familiar melodies.[4]

When children use the sound of their voices in expressive ways during pretend play (as described on p. 48), it often turns into humming and singing. They may repeat the same notes and phrases over and over. Or they may "sing" a commentary about what they are doing.

Before recall time, Fariyal sings "Open, Shut Them" and does the hand motions.

❖

At work time in the block area, Jason makes up this song as he hammers golf tees into Styrofoam: "Bang, bang, bang it hard. Down it goes. Down it goes. Wham! Bam!"

❖

At work time in the house area, Sally makes up this song as she rocks her doll to sleep in the cradle: "Close your eyes. Gonna drink some milk. The kitty is sleeping too."

Developing a sense of melody

By putting together bits and pieces of familiar songs, or making up their own, children develop a sense of melody. You can support this awareness in several ways. For example, sing a melody without words, using a neutral syllable such as "bah." This is helpful for introducing a new song as well as for working with children with limited vocabulary or who are English language learners. Once they learn the melody this way, it is easier for them to add words.

[4]Music educators use the term "random pitch" to describe singing notes without concern for the "correctness" of the pitch. Random pitch allows children and adults to sing in whatever range the children find comfortable, without worrying about hitting the "right" note or singing in the key in which a melody was written. Children often sing in random pitch when they make up songs during pretend play. As they learn and repeat familiar songs, their pitch becomes more accurate.

Another strategy is to join in when you hear children singing (but be careful not to take over the singing or children may stop). An adult voice helps to stabilize the children's pitch and they can follow along. Or, sing the first few notes of a familiar song and wait for the children to chime in. Encourage children to make up their own words to familiar songs, such as a rhyming word at the end of a line ("Hickory, dickory, dee. The mouse ran up the tree"), or an alliterative word at the beginning of a line ("Ga, ga, green sheep"). Model these word changes yourself until the children get the idea, then let them make suggestions for others to try. In addition to exercising their singing voices, children will also be developing literacy skills in phonological awareness (KDI 24. Phonological awareness).

At large-group time, when it is her turn to make up the words, Amelia sings, "Row, row, row your boat, gently down the sand. Merrily, merrily, merrily, merrily, life is but a hand."

❖

At outside time with their hands joined, Franklin and Colin chant, "Bing around the bosie" to the tune of "Ring Around the Rosie."

Play a wide variety of recorded and live music

Children benefit from hearing a wide range of musical styles, both instrumental and vocal. Offer an assortment that includes folk music from around the world, classical music, jazz and modern music, march and circus music, and waltzes, tangos, and ballets. Play primarily instrumental rather than vocal music so children are not distracted by the words. (The brain attends to language first and prevents them from hearing other aspects of the music, such as tempo or instrumentation.) Be sure to include music that is representative of local cultures and communities. Invite family members to loan the class their favorite musical recordings.

Live music is also a special treat for everyone, adults and children alike. Teachers, other staff members, parents, and musicians from the community can all provide music in the classroom. The instruments do not need to be sophisticated, nor the music complex. Even a harmonica or drums can be used with young children to explore melody, beat, and other musical properties. Arrange a field trip to a local middle or high school to listen to their band or orchestra (a child may have an older siblings in one of these groups). Not only will the preschoolers enjoy the live performance, but it is also a boost for the older students to have an appreciative audience.

Just as singing can occur at many times during the daily routine, so can playing instrumental music. Children can listen and move to music at large-group time or draw and paint to music at small-group time. Again, remember to play instrumental selections at these times because lyrics distract children from their other purposeful actions. Children may also choose to listen to music at work time in a quiet part of the room. Playing music is also a good way to cue and accompany children's movements during transitions.

While music can be a meaningful element in many parts of the daily routine, do not play music as "background noise" throughout the day. Constant music can be distracting and make it harder for children to focus on their own thoughts and actions. Background music can also interfere with conversation, hindering both listeners and speakers. Treating music as background noise also works against active engagement with and attention to music's unique and valuable qualities.

Provide simple instruments

Preschoolers enjoy playing simple musical instruments, especially percussive ones that involve active hand and body movements. These can include wooden blocks and sticks, drums, bells, xylophones, tambourines, triangles, maracas, washboards, and pots and spoons. Be sure to provide instruments that can be played one in each hand, such as jingle bells, rhythm sticks, and egg shakers. Also, include instruments that reflect the children's cultures, such as simple stringed instruments or gourds. You can also offer — and have children create — various homemade noisemakers by filling containers and taping the ends or the lids shut. For example, fill metal, wooden, cardboard, or cloth containers with beads, pebbles, sand, metal washers, or wood chips. If your program's policies permit, you can also use dried foods such as beans, pasta, or rice as filler materials.

At work time in the music area, Eddie sets up the band drums and some other percussion instruments in the style of a drum set. He sits on the floor and uses his hand to play various patterns: alternating loud and soft, or fast and slow drum beats. Then he gets a wooden stick and experiments with rubbing and rolling it across the top of the drums.

Children enjoy playing these instruments on their own, for example, at work or outside time. You can also introduce them at small- and large-group times. Children might choose to play them as they sing a familiar song, parade around the playground, or provide the music for a pretend trip to outer space as they travel on a spaceship they made with blocks. Another option is to divide the group in half, so one group plays the instruments while the other moves to the sound, then switch roles. Instruments are also a good way to signal transition times. Some story characters can be represented with instruments, for example, playing different pitches on the xylophone for the baby, mama, and papa bear (high, medium, and low, respectively) or asking the children to choose an instrument for each creature in "Where the Wild Things Are."

At work time in the music area, Sarah plays the scale up and down on the xylophone.

❖

At small-group time, after making a "rubber band" guitar, Nell sings a song while strumming on the rubber bands. She says, "the blue one makes quiet sounds, this one makes rubber band sounds." Joshua also makes up a song about guitars as he strums on the rubber bands. He sings: "Rock the band. Rock the band. I'm the singer king."

Children can use musical instruments imaginatively during many parts of the daily routine.

❖

At small-group time, Lanie and Louie tape together small twigs and branches to make their own "flutes." First they "blow" different pitches. When Lanie says, "Play faster," they take shallow breaths and blow notes as quickly as they can. Finally, they blow a long, fading note. [The children actually "hum" rather than "blow" the notes.]

Musical instruments can enrich the stop-and-start games that help children develop mathematical concepts about measuring time (KDI 36. Measuring). For example, musical chairs can be played to a drum (or other instrument), played by the teacher or a child. This game is appropriate for preschoolers as long as there are no winners and losers, that is, the focus is simply on everyone finding a chair when the leader stops playing the instrument. Finally, transitions can be accompanied by musical instruments; for example, a teacher or child might play one to signal the beginning of cleanup time.

For examples of how children explore skills and concepts in music, and how adults can support and gently extend musical learning at different levels of development, see "Ideas for Scaffolding KDI. 41 Music." You can apply these ideas in addition to those already described in your music-related play and interactions with the children in your program.

Ideas for Scaffolding KDI 41. Music

Always support children at their current level and occasionally offer a gentle extension.

Earlier	Middle	Later
Children may • Listen to sounds in the environment (e.g., stop what they are doing when a loud truck goes by); use classroom materials (e.g., pots, pans, car keys) to make sounds; attempt to copy sounds (e.g., siren of a passing fire engine). • Observe (listen to) others singing; occasionally participate (e.g., babble along; sing a word or phrase); do a few accompanying movements.	*Children may* • Label sounds (e.g., "That's the bell for cleanup time"); add sounds to the items they play with (e.g., car noises; doll baby cries); play different instruments. • Sing simple familiar songs (e.g., "Row, Row, Row Your Boat"); sing all or most of the words to the refrain or chorus (e.g., "Jingle Bells" chorus); do most accompanying movements.	*Children may* • Describe sounds in the environment (e.g., wind makes a "whooshing" noise; thunder goes "boom"; helicopter blades "whirr"); experiment with properties of sound such as fast/slow and loud/soft (e.g., tap a drum with different things to explore loudness; fill shakers to listen to the sounds made by different materials). • Sing complex songs; sing chorus and verses; create and sing simple songs while they play (e.g., sing "Go to sleep baby. Go to sleep").
To support children's current level, adults can • Call children's attention to sounds inside and outside the classroom (e.g., "Listen. I hear the train whistle"); imitate the sounds children copy (e.g., the sounds of toys, vehicles, and household items). • Sing with children throughout the day; encourage them to participate but accept if they choose to listen.	***To support children's current level, adults can*** • Encourage children to name the sounds they hear; provide instruments that make a variety of sounds (e.g., tambourine, wood blocks, triangles, rhythm sticks). • Include simple songs in the class songbook; ask children to choose what songs to sing (e.g., "Sonia, it's your turn to pick a song from the songbook").	***To support children's current level, adults can*** • Repeat the words children use to describe environmental sounds. • Substitute words in songs; make up words to familiar tunes (e.g., to the tune of "Did You Ever See a Lassie," sing "It's time to do cleanup, do cleanup, do cleanup").
To offer a gentle extension, adults can • Guess environmental sounds with children; provide sound-making materials for them to explore. • Model and encourage children to sing one or two words such as where they will play (e.g., sing "Where are you going?" and they sing back "House area") or what they are doing (e.g., while they hammer, sing "Bing, bang, bing, bang").	***To offer a gentle extension, adults can*** • Introduce new vocabulary words to label sounds (e.g., *clang, whistle, hum, whoosh*). • Gradually introduce more complicated songs and fingerplays during the year (e.g., songs with two verses or several movements).	***To offer a gentle extension, adults can*** • Comment on the sounds children create during play (e.g., "You made your train go clang!"); encourage them to create other sounds (e.g., "I wonder what noise the baby will make in the bath"). • Encourage children to change words in familiar songs (e.g., "What else crawls up a water spout?") and to create songs (e.g., "How can we sing 'Put on your coat'?").

CHAPTER 5

KDI 42. Movement

F. Creative Arts

42. Movement: Children express and represent what they observe, think, imagine, and feel through movement.

Description: Children explore moving their whole bodies, or parts of their bodies, with and without music. They respond to the features and moods of music through movement.

At large-group time, Aimee waves a scarf fast and slow as the musical selections change. For slow music, she waves it side to side above her head. When fast music plays, she waves it up and down in front of her. On the next-to-last selection, which is the fastest, she spins around. When her teacher announces that she's going to play the final piece of music, which is also the slowest, Aimee gently waves her scarf and lowers it to the floor.

❖

At work time in the block area, Cincia balances walking along a long, flat block. "If I fall off, she tells her teacher Joyce, "the alligators will get me!"

❖

At cleanup time, Michelle (the teacher) asks, "How can we move the blocks across the room with just our feet?" The children try sliding the blocks with their feet, holding blocks between their feet and shuffling across the room, and balancing the blocks on top of their feet.

❖

At outside time, Sloan walks around all the corners of the sandbox, dragging his feet. Yiyun follows behind him, copying his style of walking. As they reach each corner, they tap it with their toes and count off together, "One, two, three, four." On the third circuit, Yiyun suggests they count higher and she takes the lead, "Five, six, seven, eight." After a few more rounds, they switch directions and begin counting again at "one."

As their bodies continue to develop and they gain greater motor control, young children go beyond just using their bodies in functional ways. They also take great pleasure in expressing themselves through creative movement, that is, "taking a familiar movement and changing it in some way" (Sawyers, Colley, & Icaza, 2010, p. 32). When teachers accept and share children's delight in stretching the boundaries of what their bodies can do — without judging or comparing their efforts to anyone else's — preschoolers experiment, invent, and try new ways to move in the course of their play. They eagerly take up the suggestions of adults, rise to challenges, and copy one another's movements during small- and large-group activities.

How Movement Develops

Basic and creative movement

While toddlers are still mastering the basics of movement, preschoolers are freer to push the limits of their bodies in new and creative ways. As they explore the physical and imaginative possibilities, children are aided by the fact that movement provides its own instant feedback. Children know when their attempts are working — they remain upright, get where they want to go, or enjoy seeing their gestures appropriately interpreted by others. Likewise, children sense when they need to modify their movements — they lose their balance, miss their destination, or don't quite get across the idea their faces and bodies are trying to convey. To their delight, it only takes inventiveness and determination to come up with new or better ways of moving.

Here are some of the creative ways you may see preschool children move:

At large-group time, Kendra holds her arms tight against her sides and stands in the middle of a carpet square "so the hot lava won't burn me."

❖

At outside time, Willa runs in zigzags across the yard.

❖

At outside time, Andrew stands on the tire and swings forward and back, then tries to bounce and swing at the same time. "Look, Beth, I'm jiggling!" he calls excitedly to his teacher. When she comes over to watch, Andrew explains, "You have to bend your knees a lot of times."

❖

At work time in the book area, David jumps up and down to a steady beat while counting from 1 to 10 as he plays a computer math game.

Preschoolers enjoy feeling a freedom of movement in the play space.

Despite this seeming variety, research shows young children can be quite limited in the types of creative movement they use (Sims, 1985). For example, while listening to music, three-year-olds are likely to move in place, while four- and five-year-olds use locomotor movements but limit them to a few repetitive patterns (e.g., up and down, side to side, or circular). However, the variety of children's movements can increase if adults intentionally introduce new ideas and encourage uninhibited experimentation. For example, when adults model different body postures, actions, and hand gestures, children demonstrate a wider range of movements in response to music and also as a general means of creative expression (Stellaccio & McCarthy, 1999).

Movement as a form of representation

Preschool children can also move based on their own mental images of, for example, giants, horses, balloons, climbing a ladder, or driving a car. Their ability to represent enables them to use the language of movement as a form of expression along with speaking, art, music, and pretend play. Conveying their feelings, experiences, and ideas through movement builds young children's confidence in their ability to communicate with their bodies.

At greeting circle, Brian moves his arms up and down to show his teacher Sam how the owl he saw the previous evening with his dad flew across the sky.

❖

At work time in the house area, Dakota and Rosie curl their bodies into balls and crawl under a blanket like "sleeping baby chicks."

❖

At large-group time, the children figure out ways to sink to the floor slowly like falling leaves.

❖

At work time, going from the block area to the art area, Holly walks heel-to-toe across the room with her arms stretched to the side. She tells her teacher, "This is my ballerina walk."

❖

At greeting circle, Andreas wiggles his fingers like the fringe on his new cowboy vest.

This sense of bodily comfort and creativity in movement spills over into other areas of learning and strengthens children's belief in themselves as academically capable, socially competent, and imaginative young people (Centers for Disease Control, 2010). In fact, like all the other creative arts, expressive movement can be connected to virtually every area of the preschool curriculum. Educator Mimi Chenfeld says poetically, "During the 47 years I've been bouncing around the education field, we have danced and moved to depict…all the king's horses racing to help Humpty Dumpty; the transformations of caterpillar to butterfly, tadpole to frog; the dynamic pageant of moving seasons; the wheels of the bus on the way to the zoo; number facts and spelling words….Every idea is a universe of possibilities" (2005, pp. 50–51).

Teaching Strategies That Support Movement

Children express themselves through movement, sometimes contorting their bodies in almost unimaginable ways. It is important that preschoolers feel comfortable experimenting with all types of positions and actions, knowing adults will accept and share their delight in this exuberant experimentation. Movement educator Phyllis Weikart emphasizes that "expressing creativity through movement is not a one-time experience. Creative movement cannot be 'taught' at a specific time or place. Rather, it evolves over time when children are in the care of adults who consistently promote and support [it] as children explore, plan, make choices, initiate ideas, lead other children, work cooperatively, and solve problems" (2000, p. 111). To encourage children's ongoing explorations with creative movement, use the following teaching strategies.

Describe and encourage children to describe their creative use of movement

Notice the spontaneous ways that children express themselves with movement throughout the day, and support their actions by commenting on what they are doing. For example, during work time you might see a child moving unusually with an object and say, "You're stepping slowly so the scarf doesn't fall off your head." At cleanup time, note how children carry objects back to their place of storage: "Justin is walking tippy-toe on his way to the puzzle shelf." At large-group time, label children's movements and encourage others to imitate them: "Jonathan and Luke are flapping their arms like birds. I'm going to try that too." Comments like these let children know their explorations with creative movement are important and merit attention.

At large-group time, Jeremiah waves his arms from side to side over his head to show how the wind shakes the tree branches just outside the classroom window. "You're moving your arms like the limbs of the tree in the wind," notes his teacher, imitating his action. Several other children begin to wave their arms above their heads the same way. "We're all being trees," says Jeremiah, clearly pleased that others are copying the movement he invented.

❖

At outside time, listening to music on the portable CD player, Charlotte moves across the grass with streamers. "Look, I'm twirling," she tells Isobel, her teacher. "You're twirling around and around," acknowledges Isobel. "Now I'm going up and down, like the horse on the merry-go-round." Isobel repeats "Up and down, up and down" as Charlotte raises and lowers not just her arms, but her whole body, to make the streamers flutter.

Talking with children about their creative movements also helps them become more conscious of what they are doing, and lets them be more deliberate in their actions. Having the language to describe and reflect on a wide variety of movements expands preschoolers' abilities to represent their thoughts and feelings, and to use their bodies to solve problems encountered in play.

At large-group time, Julie (a teacher) plays the guitar, stops, then plays again. While she plays, the children move their arms to the music. When she stops playing, they stop moving. When she resumes playing, the children move their arms a different way. During the "stop" time she comments, "You moved your arms in all kinds of ways!" The children respond as follows: "I waved mine around"; "I bounced mine up and down like you played the guitar"; "My arms bended like a straw"; "I made mine go faster than anything!"; "I waved to you!"

❖

At large-group time, when it is her turn to suggest a way to move, Nikki says, "Run around the circle." Gavin's idea is that "Everybody should hop"; Sam says, "Crawl on our knees"; and Rosie suggests "Let's all walk backwards!"

❖

At work time in the house area, Philippa has trouble carrying three dolls in her arms at once from the table to the carriage. She drapes one doll over each shoulder and cradles the third in front of her, walking very slowly so the ones on her shoulders do not fall off. When she arrives at the carriage, she shrugs the dolls off her shoulders and puts the third one inside too. After she arranges them and covers them with a blanket, she sighs with relief and satisfaction.

Young children need to feel comfortable experimenting with movement, knowing that adults accept and will talk with them about their experimentations.

Encourage children to solve movement problems at group times and transitions

While children generate and solve their own movement problems as they play, they also enjoy solving interesting movement challenges that adults set for them. In addition to being fun for everyone, adults can use these activities as a way to introduce new movement ideas that children can experiment with on their own throughout the day. Intriguing suggestions from adults not only increase the child's repertoire of creative movements, but also the vocabulary that accompanies them.

You can invent movement problems at any time of the day, but they are especially appropriate at small- and large-group times, to build on children's explorations at outside time, and as a useful strategy to help transitions go smoothly. The ideas can come from anywhere, including the ways you see children move during play, movements described in familiar books and nursery rhymes, or observations of how mechanical objects and things in nature move. Here are some examples:

At cleanup time, when the children's enthusiasm flags, Beth says, "I saw Julia picking up blocks with her elbows. I wonder if we could put away all the blocks just using our elbows."

❖

At large-group time, Erik says, "I wonder how you would move if you were a cow jumping over the moon."

❖

At the end of greeting circle, Peter asks the children "How could we move to planning time without walking?"

❖

At large-group time Julie sits on the floor with the children and puts a beanbag on her head. The children laugh. "Where besides my head could I put it?" she asks them. "On your knee," Anderson suggests, and Julie carries out his idea. Then she gives each child a beanbag and says, "See if you can put it on your knee." After balancing beanbags on their knees and heads, the children experiment with other places: palms, elbows, shoulders, backs, cheeks, and toes.

This child figures out how to balance on some blocks.

Provide opportunities for children to represent their experiences through movement

Because preschoolers are able to represent objects, feelings, and actions, they can move their bodies in ways that reflect their personal experiences. Just as they talk, draw, or sing about what they have done, so they can also use creative movement to describe past actions or represent what they imagine could happen. For example, at recall time, ask children to demonstrate what they did at work time just using their hands or their bodies. Here is what one group of children did:

Mikey moved his fingers to show how he had worked at the computer.

❖

Ben made painting and cutting motions.

❖

Callie and Aimee lay on the floor and showed how they covered themselves up with a blanket.

❖

Anna and Jessa flew and buzzed like bees.

❖

Kenneth made small movements with his hands to show how he put together Legos.

You can encourage children to use their bodies to express familiar emotions, such as feelings of being sad, mad, frightened, brave, friendly, shy, and silly. For example, you might say, "How do you move your body when you are feeling happy?" or "Let's move to the snack table as though we're tired and sleepy." Ask children to suggest other feelings the group can represent with their bodies. Think of characters in familiar books, and encourage the children to move in ways that match how they felt at key points in the narrative: "I wonder how Max (in *Where the Wild Things Are* by Maurice Sendak) moved when he came home and found his dinner was still warm."

Children also enjoy representing field trips using creative movement. For example, one preschool group in New England went to the town square for a local harvest celebration. When they came back to the classroom and recalled their trip, it quickly became clear to the teachers that what the children were most interested in was the bus trip. "How could we show what it was like on the bus just using our bodies?" they asked. After some discussion, the children sat down in pairs and swayed from side to side while the "driver" in the front steered around one sharp corner after another. They took turns being the driver, twisting their arms back and forth in a circular motion. These simple movements allowed the children to capture the highlight of their trip.

Use other times of the daily routine to encourage children to represent their experiences. For example, during transitions, the children can move like objects or animals. Depending on what they are familiar with, ask them to go to the playground, lunchroom, or their cots while moving as if they were trees in the wind, a frisky puppy, a ball, or a blinking neon sign. When appropriate, you can also use these representational movement ideas to build on other recent activities the children have enjoyed. For example, after a small-group time in which children "fished" for and counted numbered fishes using magnetic wands, one teacher encouraged them to move like fishes to snacktime. After reading *The Snowy Day* by Ezra Jack Keats at another small-group time, the children were excited to see how many types of snow angels they could make at outside time.

This child gestures with movement as she recalls what she did at work time.

Encourage simple ways of moving creatively to music

When young children hear live or recorded music, they naturally want to move to it. Having a variety of musical styles in the classroom encourages them to move in different ways, such as fast and slow, bouncy or smooth, intense or relaxed, swaying or marching, and with their bodies up high or down low. Providing props such as scarves, streamers, paper plates, rhythm sticks, and other percussion instruments also encourages young children to move in creative ways as they listen to and enjoy the various qualities of music, such as tempo, pitch, and volume.

Playing music in the classroom encourages children to move in a variety of ways.

Imitate children's expressive movements (for example, "I'm going to try moving just like you are"). Call children's attention to the creative movements of their peers and comment specifically on how it is connected to the quality of the music: "Sammy is swinging his arms back and forth in time to the lively beat"; "Eleanor is sliding across the floor to the smooth-sounding music." You can also create simple movement sequences to music together with children. For example, take a song with two parts (such as "Yankee Doodle") and encourage them to do a different movement for each. In this case, they might decide to march to the verse and wave their arms to the chorus.

At large-group time, Marcus waves his arms in the air as he skates to the music.

❖

At large-group time, Vanna stomps across the floor to the fast music. When the music changes to a slower tempo, she switches to a gliding movement.

❖

At large-group time, Caleb suggests that everybody march around the blue carpet as they play rhythm sticks. He calls it a parade.

For examples of how preschool children discover and experiment with creative movement at different stages of development, and the strategies adults can use to support and gently extend their learning, see "Ideas for Scaffolding KDI. 42 Movement" on page 66. The additional ideas in the chart, together with those described above, can be used in play and other interactions with children throughout your program's daily routine.

Ideas for Scaffolding KDI 42. Movement

Always support children at their current level and occasionally offer a gentle extension.

Earlier	Middle	Later
Children may • Explore moving their bodies or parts of their bodies. • Move their bodies independently of the features (tempo or mood) of the music (e.g., run fast to slow music).	*Children may* • Use movement to represent their experiences in simple ways (e.g., flap their arms like a bird). • Move in one or two ways connected to the music (e.g., march to the beat; jump up and down to lively music).	*Children may* • Use movement to represent their experiences in complex ways (e.g., twirl around and sway back and forth like a leaf blowing in the wind). • Describe how their movements are connected to the features of the music (e.g., "I'm moving slowly because this is floaty music").
To support children's current level, adults can • Provide opportunities for children to move their bodies throughout the day in addition to large-group and outside time. • Play many types of music for children to move to; accept and encourage children to move in any way they want to the music.	*To support children's current level, adults can* • Imitate children's expressive movements (e.g., "I'm moving like a sad puppy, just like you"). • Describe your own and children's movements in relation to the music (e.g., "I'm tiptoeing when the music is soft"; "You're bouncing to the lively music").	*To support children's current level, adults can* • Describe children's complex movements (e.g., "You're crossing your arms and stomping hard to show how angry the monster is!"). • Provide a variety of musical features for children to move to (e.g., staccato, smooth, jazzy, waltz tempo; major and minor keys); describe the music and their own accompanying movements (e.g., "This is eerie music so I'm creeping on the ground").
To offer a gentle extension, adults can • Label their own and children's movements (e.g., "I'm flapping my arms"; "You're stretching"). • Imitate and describe how other children move to music (e.g., "I'm swaying to the music like Justin").	*To offer a gentle extension, adults can* • Encourage children to move in a way they did at work time or during another recent activity. • Ask children to describe their movements and how they relate to the music (e.g., "What about the music makes you want to move that way?").	*To offer a gentle extension, adults can* • Encourage children to move in an imaginary situation (e.g., "On our way to the rug, let's move like someone spilled glue on the floor"; "How would the Papa Bear move to the snack table?"). • Ask children to describe how their movements differ with contrasting musical styles (e.g., "How did you move differently when the music changed?").

CHAPTER 6

KDI 43. Pretend Play

F. Creative Arts

43. Pretend play: Children express and represent what they observe, think, imagine, and feel through pretend play.

Description: Children imitate actions, use one object to stand for another, and take on roles themselves based on their interests and experiences. They use figures to represent characters in their pretend scenarios (e.g., having a "family" of toy bears talk to one another). Their play themes develop in detail and complexity over time.

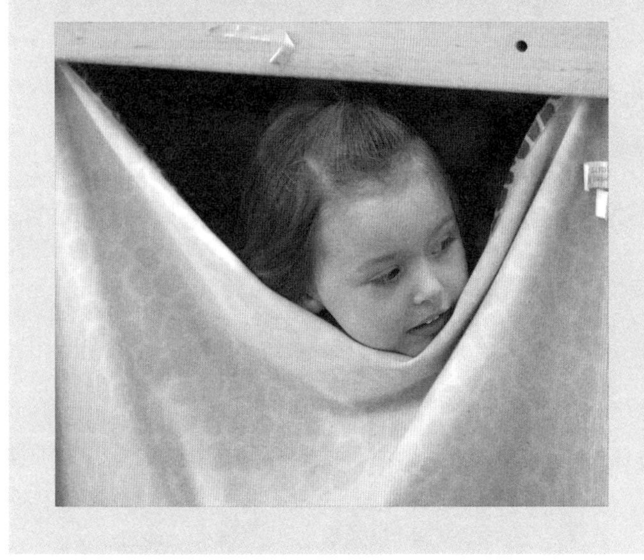

At work time in the art area, Kacey asks the kitty puppet, "Do you want some milk?" "Meow! Yes! Lots of warm milk," she makes the puppet answer in a high voice.

❖

At work time in the block area, Kai and Scarlett pretend to be the superheroes Batman and Robin. They cut sheets of butcher paper in the art area and staple strings at the corners to tie them as "bat capes" around their necks. "We gotta catch the bad guys!" says Kai. "They're robbers!" confirms Scarlett, as they spread out their capes and fly around the room.

❖

During the transition from snacktime to large-group time, Joey walks on his hands and feet. "Look! I can walk like a spider!" he says to his teacher.

❖

At large-group time, Kresley strums his hands in imitation of his teacher playing the guitar.

How Pretend Play Develops

Pretend play — also called sociodramatic play — involves both imitation and imagination. When young children imitate, they use gestures, sounds, words, and props to represent the world they know. In imaginative play, preschoolers express their fantasies about a world that could be. They act out the "what if's..." inside their minds, carry out their intentions alone or with others, and reveal their emotions. As they represent what they see, hear, think, and feel, preschoolers make sense of the people and events in their lives. They are increasingly able to differentiate reality from fantasy, based on their cumulative experiences. Re-creating or modifying real and imagined experiences also helps children understand and feel a sense of control over their environment.

At work time in the house area, Ella, Talia, and Sue (a teacher) play together with the dolls. Talia pretends to be the doctor and Ella pretends to be the pharmacist. Sue takes prescriptions from Talia and gives them to Ella. Ella fills bottles with sand and gives them back to Sue.

The purpose of pretend play is discovery and exploration, not performance—just as it is in the other areas of creative arts. Preschoolers explore using materials, and their voices and bodies, to express their thoughts and perceptions. Pretend play is also inherently social. Children interact with one another and partnering adults, contributing ideas and building on the ideas of others.

The importance of pretend play

Psychologists have pondered the importance of pretend play in early development for decades. Jean Piaget (1951/1962) believed it strengthened children's growing ability to mentally picture situations and take control over experiences in which they had little say (such as going to the doctor). Vygotsky (1978) saw the roles and rules that children invent in dramatic play as supporting their emerging self-regulation. In their desire to remain part of the play scenario, children pay attention to the behaviors and emotions of others and adjust their own behavior accordingly.

Research supports both these theories. Pretend play strengthens children's skills in attention, memory, reasoning, language, imagination, and emotional understanding. It allows them to reflect on their own thinking, take another's perspective, inhibit impulses, and control their behavior (Tomlinson & Hyson, 2009). Adults can also help children with less-developed social skills enter the pretend play of their peers (KDI 13. Cooperative play).

At work time in the block area, Kovid and Joshua talk as though they are the dinosaurs they are playing with. Kovid says in his deepest voice, "My name is Anthony." Josh makes his dinosaur ask, ""What do you want to do?" Kovid replies, "I want to fight." Josh says, "No way! We will have a talk about that." Kovid then says, "That one wants to kill us" and points to a third dinosaur. Josh answers, "No, let's get away." Kovid holds up another dinosaur and says, "This is Robert." Josh asks, "Is he nice?" and Kovid replies, "Yeah, but he is sleeping."

Research shows that social behavior is more mature and reciprocal in pretend play than in non-pretend activities. Observing the spontaneous pretend play of preschoolers, Judith Chafel (1984) found they often sought confirmation from one another with conventional statements such as "OK?" "See?" "Right?" and "Don't we?" Children move outside the play frame for these brief interpersonal negotiations to keep the play going, then return to the pretend action itself. In this way, play is both a means of creative expression and a way to promote social development.

At work time in the block area, Douglas tells Brian and Sarah, "I'm Santa Claus. It's Christmas Eve. Everybody go to sleep!" Brian and Sarah lie on the floor, cover themselves with scarves, close their eyes, and pretend to sleep. "Now you have to give us presents," says Brian. After some discussion, the three children decide the presents will be crayons, and they bring back a basketful from the art area. "Back to sleep boys and girls," orders Douglas. When Brian and Sarah lie down again, Douglas puts several crayons beside each of them.

Professor Doris Fromberg says, "There is a consensus that sociodramatic play influences social competence. In general, social and moral development take place as young children interact with others. The social negotiations of pretend play are a particularly potent and influential realm of experience" (1999, p. 35). In addition, pretend play can contribute significantly to children's cognitive development. This is especially true when the imagined activity is scaffolded by adults who act as partners to sustain and extend the children's play scenario (Bodrova & Leong, 2007). For example, teachers can help children plan what they will play, think about the roles they and their friends might take,

Pretend play is inherently social and helps children develop social competence.

decide what props they want to use, anticipate the problems they might encounter carrying out their ideas, and consider how they might go about solving them.

Types of pretend play

Pretend play begins at about 18 months, as children imitate the actions and sounds of familiar people, animals, objects, and situations. Parallel play (playing *alongside* others) arises in the second year, and becomes social (playing *with* others) at around age three. During the preschool years, as children's representational abilities increase, pretend play also becomes more imaginative and imitative. Children use props more elaborately, moving from using one object to stand for something similar (pretending a small rectangular block is a cell phone or a plate is a steering wheel) to creating objects that support complex play themes (putting up a sign, coloring place mats, and writing menus to play restaurant).

At work time in the house area, Ellie and Gabrielle play kitties inside the "kitty hotel" they have built with blocks. They lie on the pillows, meowing and crawling around.

❖

At work time in the house area, Christian, Jacob, and Lute pretend to be firefighters. Jacob calls Christian on the telephone to help put out the fire. "Quick, it's burning really fast," he urges. Lute, making a siren noise, follows with a length of hose to spray his "chemicals."

Compared to toddlers, preschoolers' pretend play can be quite sophisticated (Kavanaugh, 2006). As noted above, the use of props becomes more flexible and detailed. Play scenarios become less self-centered and increasingly involve others; for example, instead of just pretending to eat a play dough pizza, the child may also offer a slice to someone else. By age four, children collaborate with one or more peers to create a scene with multiple roles and story lines (a mother takes her sick baby to the hospital where the doctor gives it a shot and medicine). "Make-believe or pretend play, with guidance and support from adults, blossoms in the preschool years....Other types of play, such as drawing or doing puzzles, are important too. But there is something special about social pretend play for preschoolers [with] important benefits for children's cognitive (and other types of) development" (Tomlinson & Hyson, 2009, p. 130).

At work time in the house area, Tony puts a baby doll in the high chair and feeds it "cereal" (pebbles) from a bowl. He tells his teacher, "Evan (his baby brother) eats cereal. He likes milk."

❖

At work time in the house area, Malcolm pretends to make chai tea for his teacher Sue. He puts on an oven mitt and says, "It's going to be hot so I have to wear a glove." When the tea is done, Malcolm blows into the cup to cool it off before he hands it to Sue.

❖

At work time in the toy area, Matthew, Josh, and Nevaeh use the Lego blocks and people. They each build a house and talk in the voice of the Lego people as they visit one another. "Let's pretend we're having a potluck dinner," Matthew suggests. The others like this idea, and they each tell what kinds of food they are bringing — tacos, pie, watermelon, hot dogs, and noodles.

Studies show that when they engage in mature sociodramatic play — that is, pretend play that involves communication with others — children's interactions last longer than they do in other social situations, they show higher levels of sustained involvement, more children are drawn into the play scenario, and children also show more cooperation and negotiation with one another (Creasey, Jarvis, & Berk, 1998). Children play creatively for longer periods of time and with greater complexity as they get older, but even younger children engage in more complex play when interacting with older peers and adults (Brownell, 1990).

By age six, however, pretend play often declines (Cole & LaVoie, 1985). One reason is that imagination becomes more internalized. Children entertain "what if" thoughts in their mind without needing to act them out. They may also be responding to elementary-age pressures to incorporate an academic focus in the play. For example, they may practice writing skills to "play school," or measure to build a space station, rather than invent scenarios outside the realm of reality. The preschool years are therefore especially critical to establishing play's creative roots, so children can return to and build upon them in adolescence and adulthood. At this later point, they will be ready to apply the cognitive skills that are by then fully developed in the service of expressing their imaginations.

Teaching Strategies That Support Pretend Play

Preschoolers engage in pretend play when they imitate the actions and sounds they encounter in everyday life and imagine scenarios that take familiar experiences in new directions. Pretend play occurs alone and with peers, and is especially enriched when adults play as partners in the dramas children create. To promote children's pretend play, use the strategies described below.

Support children as they imitate what they see and hear

Children use their bodies and voices to imitate or reproduce the actions and sounds around them — a puppy crawling on all fours, laundry flapping in the wind, the whistle of a train, or a baby crying. You can support this type of pretend play by in turn imitating what the children do. For example, if a child "meows" and pretends to lap milk from a bowl on the floor, you can "meow," get down beside them and make lapping sounds and motions too.

Using steering wheels, these children imitate the automobile-driving behavior of the adults in their lives.

Imitating children's action may lead to an "action dialogue" — communication carried out with gestures instead of words.

At work time in the house area, Timmy stands in front of the mirror and strokes his cheeks with a small rubber spatula as he pretends to shave.

❖

At work time in the toy area, Brandon snaps together two blocks and flies them over his head, making an "airplane noise."

❖

At work time in the house area, Roseanna plays babies with her teacher Sybil. Roseanna packs a suitcase with baby things, and they carry their baby dolls to the art area for a "meeting." Roseanna writes on paper at the "meeting" and gives paper and pencil to Sybil so she can also "take notes." Whenever Roseanna writes something on her paper, Sybil does too.

❖

At work time in the block area, Jaye announces she is leading an aerobics class. She stretches her arms high over her head. Her teacher Gary imitates her stretching action. When Jaye kicks one foot and then the other forward, Gary does the same. After she performs each part of the exercise routine — bending, twisting, and so on — Jaye pauses and looks at Gary to see if he will imitate her. Only after he reproduces each of her actions does Jaye go on to the next one.

In addition to work time, take advantage of other opportunities for imitation throughout the day. For example, at recall time, children can pantomime what they did at work time, such as pretend to read a book, paint at the easel, or stack blocks. After you read a book at the end of snacktime, children can imitate the actions of the characters in the story (for example, growl like a monster). They can imitate movements in the songs they sing at large-group time ("row" a boat) or make up new verses and accompanying actions ("This is the way we brush our hair").

At recall time, Gretchen shows how she used the computer keyboard at work time by making typing motions with her fingers.

❖

At large-group time, Randy lifts one leg at a time while the other children sing and mime, "This is the way we put on our pajamas."

Imitation, especially of unexpected movements or sounds, can also make cleanup fun. For example, when Andee walked backwards to put away the blocks, her teacher Jeannette copied her movements. Soon, the entire class declared it a "backwards cleanup day." On another occasion, Charles "flew" each item to the shelf and made buzzing airplane sounds as he put away the toys. His teacher imitated both the gestures and noises while cleaning up alongside him.

Children also see and hear new things to imitate on field trips. A good way to recall and reflect on these experiences is to have children re-create the actions and sounds that were meaningful to them. Children will spontaneously imitate what they saw and heard. You can also initiate this activity on the ride back to the classroom, at snacktime, or in a follow-up small-group activity.

The class goes on a field trip to the zoo where they visit the Penguin House. At work time at the water table the next day, Dahlia uses small dinosaur figures and says, "I'm pretending they're penguins." She walks them around the edge of the water table and then makes them flop head-first into the water. She says, "They are swimming and diving."

Watch for and support imaginative role play throughout the classroom

Provide space and materials for pretending and role play. For example, equipment and dress-up clothes in the house area might inspire children to act out a family dinner table scene, open a restaurant, or play office. Encourage them to create their own props as well, using materials from around the classroom. In these scenarios, children might respectively sculpt food with clay, add up the bill on a calculator, or write letters using a computer program.

At work time, at the sand table, Lynn makes "Jell-O and cakes" for her teacher Joan. She pretends to mix the cake batter and brings Joan a water-filled bowl of "white Jell-O."

❖

At work time in the house area, Theo pretends to be a doctor by wearing a stethoscope and taking care of a doll. He says, "When I get sick, I help myself because I'm a doctor."

❖

At work time in the house area, Brianna and Senguele gather the following items in their purses: paper money, keys, and phones. Senguele tells their teacher, "We're going shopping" and Brianna adds, "To Walmart, to buy bacon."

❖

At work time in the block area, Todd and Ricky put on fire hats, boots, and coats, and load their fire truck (a wagon) with a ladder (a long block) and hoses. "Briiing, briiing!" Ricky intones and answers the telephone. "Fire at Becky's!" he shouts. "Fire at Becky's!" Todd repeats. They drive the truck to the fire in the house area where Becky (their teacher) and several other children are playing. When they get there, they go "Whoosh, whoosh" with the hoses until water puts out the fire. Then they drive the truck back to the fire station.

Be alert to the people and events children portray in their role-playing activities, and provide additional materials and props to support them. For example, when several children who had gone camping with their families during summer vacation began to act out these experiences, their teachers added flashlights and a sleeping bag to the house area. Parents, informed of the children's interest, contributed a tent and a no-longer-functional cookstove.

Pretending and role play also occur outdoors. Wheeled toys (bicycles, wagons) often serve as buses, trains, airplanes, or boats. Climbing structures become houses, forts, tents, and igloos. Small items from nature, such as pebbles and leaves, are a feast for a banquet or birthday party. Bringing indoor materials (scarves, dolls, cooking utensils) outside, further helps children extend and elaborate their imaginative activities.

At outside time, Andrew pretends the climber is his rocketship. "Ten, three, five, one, blast off!" he says as he jumps into the air.

❖

At outside time in the tree house, Billy washes dishes (plastic pails, plates, and utensils from the sandbox). "I'm home, honey," Lisa calls through the window. "Okay, baby," Billy replies, "I need lettuce for the salad." Lisa picks up fallen leaves from the ground and gives them to Billy. "Here you go, honey," she says. He puts them on a plate and serves them dinner.

Large and fluid spaces also inspire children's pretend play. An open area can become whatever they want — a planet, jungle, or boat. Dramatic play often overlaps areas. For example, children in the house area may "build" a backyard barbecue in the block area. By locating these areas next to one another, you facilitate this type of creative play. Be sure children also know they can carry equipment and materials from one part of the classroom to another. This flexibility gives their imaginations free reign. In a room that is well organized and labeled, children know where to find and return all types of materials to support and extend their imaginative play.

❖

At work time in the block area, Noel builds a tent. He gets chairs from his small-group table, puts them together on the carpet, then covers them with a blanket he retrieves from the house area. He makes another tent for Colum, and says to him, "It can be anything, like a ship."

❖

At work time, Rocco pretends the pipes under the house area sink are broken. He asks the other children to leave the house area because there is sewer water all over the floor, and he needs a pump to clean it up. Rocco then gets a long block and a short block from the block area and brings them to the sink. He stands the long one on end, crosses the short one at the top, and pretends to "pump" the handles. "All clear now," he says when he's done. Rocco returns the blocks to their shelf as the other children reenter the house area.

"Let's pretend" can happen at large-group time as well, as children reenact a familiar story and/or make up one of their own. Again, these activities will be most successful if they expand on the pretend play themes that children generate spontaneously and the story ideas they are interested in from their own lives.

In addition to encouraging pretend play during regular times of the daily routine, plan special experiences to add depth to children's imaginative activities. For example, field trips expand children's horizons and give them new ideas for pretending and role play. Consider how the following memorable experience enriched a favorite pretend play scenario over time.

One day HighScope Demonstration Preschool teacher Beth Marshall (now Director of HighScope's Early Childhood department) joined three children playing "barbershop." They sat her in the barber's chair, wrapped a scarf around her shoulders, and pretended to cut her hair with scissors. Given the children's interest, Beth and her co-teacher planned a field trip to a local barbershop, where they could watch one of the children actually get a haircut. The child's parent went with them, and the teachers talked with the barber beforehand about what they wanted to happen for the children. "I suggested letting the children get into the barber chair, make the chair go up and down, feel the vibration of the electric clippers, feel the air from the blow dryer, look in the big mirror and the hand mirror, and try out the cash register" (Marshall, 1992, p. 16). In the month after the field trip, the children continued adding details to their barbershop pretend play, and more children joined in. Immediately after the trip, six children played and added the following props and actions to the original chair, scarf, and scissors: clippers, clipping noise, floor mirror, baby doll, detailed cutting, blocks for combs, and opening and closing the shop for business. Two weeks later, 13 children were

Pretending and Role Play at Large-Group Time

In a classroom in which one group of children had been pretending with "boats" made of large blocks, another group had been using a real tent to go "camping," and a third group had been playing "mermaids," the teacher built on elements from all three groups by starting a large-group time inviting the children to pretend to sail to a magic land with her.

First she asked the children to help her build a boat, which they did enthusiastically using blocks, cartons, scarves, and ropes. Then the teacher used a few planned prompts to get things started: "What should we take onboard?" and "What do we see?" After that, she followed the children's leads as the fantasy unfolded. The children discovered "jewels in a treasure chest" (buttons in a box) and swam away from sea monsters they saw with their "spyglasses" (paper towel tubes). She let them decide, again by looking through their spyglasses, when they had arrived on land.

Once there, the children continued to determine the direction of the play. They discovered a tent where "gigantic lions" were hiding out and cooked a "berry stew" (made of beads) when they got hungry. Two minutes before the end of large-group time, the teacher announced it was time for them to sail home. She again turned it over to the children to bring the voyage to closure. They braved a storm and vanquished more monsters en route, but made it back in time for snacks.

Over the next few weeks, the children incorporated and elaborated on these imaginative elements as they played "boats," "camping," "mermaids," and now, in addition, "sailing to a magic land."

playing barbershop and added these elements: telephone to make appointments, washing the doll's hair, charging and exchanging money, writing "the bill" on a pad, and a waiting area with a bench, books, and magazines.

Bringing visitors into the classroom also widens the range of experiences children can draw on in their pretend play. These can include adult family members, people from the community (artists, storekeepers, construction workers), babies (younger siblings brought in by parents), and even family pets and other animals. Because children are interested in both the physical characteristics and behaviors of these visitors, they provide an intriguing starting point for acting out roles and elaborating fantasies. Encourage visitors to leave behind props (cash register receipts or measuring tapes) that will add authenticity to the children's pretend play.

Participate as a partner in children's pretend play

Child development and theater expert Vivian Paley (1990) concludes that adults who participate as partners in children's play are better observers, understand children more, and communicate with children more effectively. However, partnering must be done with sensitivity so that children retain control of the play. Therefore observe first to understand their intentions before you join in. Wait until you are invited, or be alert to cues that the children welcome your involvement.

At work time in the house area, Dawn (a teacher) sits beside Tucker and Rona as they play "restaurant." Tucker serves Dawn chicken soup. He types letters on the computer, prints the page, and shows it to Dawn. He says it's the recipe. Dawn asks him to tell her what is in the soup.

This adult takes on a role assigned by the children in their pretend play: She will be a child and the children are the adults in her family.

After Rona asks Tucker for more soup, Dawn asks if she can have more soup too.

To make sure you respect the content and direction of the children's play, rather than "taking over," follow a simple set of guidelines. One is to continue with the play theme set by the children, for example, being another dog or baby rather than adding a new type of character. A second principle is to stay within the play situation when offering suggestions; for example, if the children are pretending to visit the doctor, do not suggest an emergency ambulance trip from the office to the hospital. A third guideline is to match the complexity of the children's play, that is, to scaffold learning at their developmental level rather than trying to "push" them to a much higher level. Finally, acknowledge and accept children's responses to your gentle ideas. If they do not pick up on them, let it go and return to the play that was happening previously. (For an example of how the teacher acted as a partner in the barbershop play, see "Four Customers, One Barber" on p. 78).

For examples of children's pretend play at different levels of development and how adults can scaffold their learning in this area of creative art, see "Ideas for Scaffolding KDI. 43 Pretend Play" on page 79. Use these ideas to carry out the foregoing strategies as you support and gently extend children's pretend play during your interactions with them across the program day.

Four Customers, One Barber

Here is how preschool teacher Beth Marshall (now Director of HighScope's Early Childhood Department) participated as a partner in children's pretend barbershop play.

One day, Douglas, Martin, and Callie were setting up the "barbershop." Callie got the clippers and scissors. Douglas and Martin wanted a haircut, and so did Corrin, who had joined them. When the three potential haircut customers began struggling over the "barber chair," Beth decided to join them: "Is this barbershop open? I think I need a trim," she said.

"Well," responded Corrin, "I think it's a problem. There's only one hair-cutting place and everybody needs to get their hair cut."

"I see," said Beth. "There's only one hair-cutting place. What do you think we should do?" (The children didn't say anything but resumed their struggle for the "barber chair.")

"Douglas could have the first turn, and then Corrin, and then you, Martin, OK?" Callie suggested.

"Well, my appointment is not for a while. I wonder what I could do while I'm waiting," Beth thought aloud.

Douglas had an idea. "We could make a waiting area!"

"Yeah, like a big bench," Corrin added. Corrin, Douglas, and Callie gathered big hollow blocks from the block area and arranged them in one long line in the "barber shop."

"Sit here on the waiting bench, Beth," Douglas instructed. Martin brought some books over, handed one to Beth, and sat down next to her. Douglas gathered some magazines from the art area, piled them on the bench, and selected one to "read." Corrin sat down in the "barber chair," Callie tied a scarf around her neck, and proceeded with the first haircut of the day. When she finished and Corrin "paid," Callie called her next customer.

"Douglas, you want to be next?" He put down his magazine and took his place in the "barber chair."

— Marshall (1992, p. 26)

Ideas for Scaffolding KDI 43. Pretend Play

Always support children at their current level and occasionally offer a gentle extension.

Earlier	Middle	Later
Children may • Pretend to be a real person, animal, or object that is familiar to them from their own lives (e.g., crawl like a cat; whirr like a motor). • Use an object to stand for another, similar object (e.g., pretend a small block is a cell phone). • Engage in pretend play on their own (e.g., imitate truck noises while racing cars up and down a ramp; hold their arms out to the sides and "fly" like an airplane).	*Children may* • Pretend to be a character in a story, song, nursery rhyme (e.g., the spider in Little Miss Muffet) or a generic role in a situation (e.g., a mom or dad feeding a baby). • Talk in the "voice" of a character when playing with people or animal figures (e.g., use a high squeaky voice for a mouse); animate figures or objects (e.g., make an airplane fly). • Engage in a simple pretend play scenario with another child (e.g., pretend to be horses together; pretend to be firefighters).	*Children may* • Pretend to be a character or play a role they imagine (e.g., "I'm the daisy fairy who gives out flowers to sick babies"). • Create a prop during pretend play (e.g., scuba gear with tubing, milk jugs for oxygen tanks, safety glasses as swim masks, paper taped to shoes as flippers). • Engage in complex play scenarios with others; step outside the role to clarify or give directions and then return to the play (e.g., say "Let's have the baby be sick. Marasol, you're the doctor. Okay, baby, mommy will take you to the doctor now," then rock and hand the doll to Marasol).
To support children's current level, adults can • Pretend with children; imitate what they say and do (e.g., meow like a cat). • Use a prop as a stand-in for the real object in the same way as the children (e.g., turn a plate like a steering wheel). • Play in parallel with children.	*To support children's current level, adults can* • Interact with children in character. • Use figures similarly to children (e.g., create an animal family with figures; talk in a different voice with your puppet). • Acknowledge when two children play together (e.g., at recall say, "Emilio, I saw you and Daryl being firefighters").	*To support children's current level, adults can* • Allow extended time for children's detailed pretend play to fully develop. • Provide materials to create props. • Ask children to assign them pretend play roles (e.g., "Okay, I'll be the ambulance driver. Tell me what to do").
To offer a gentle extension, adults can • Ask children what other features of real people, animals, and objects they can imitate (e.g., "What other sounds does your truck make?"). • Model using other materials to stand for or make familiar objects (e.g., "We could use this block for the table"). • Call children's attention to others who are pretending the same thing (e.g., "Jaron is racing his truck and going 'vroom' too").	*To offer a gentle extension, adults can* • Encourage children to add details to their roles (e.g., "What else do dads do?"). • Gently try out other voices or actions for the figures but back off if children do not pick up on them (e.g., "My plane needs to land. I need to find an airport"). • Encourage children to describe their pretend play actions to others (e.g., "Daryl, can you show Pat how you and Emilio put out your fire?").	*To offer a gentle extension, adults can* • Encourage children to imagine other scenarios (e.g., "What if there were no more sick babies for the daisy fairy?"). • Allow time for children to explore a variety of play options with the props they make (e.g., provide storage and work-in-progress signs; remind children of previous play at planning time). • Provide consistent opportunities and materials for children to elaborate their play ideas over time.

CHAPTER 7

KDI 44. Appreciating the Arts

F. Creative Arts

44. Appreciating the arts: Children appreciate the creative arts.

Description: Children express opinions and preferences about the arts. They identify the pieces (e.g., a painting or musical selection) and styles they do or do not like and offer simple explanations about why. Children describe the effects they and other artists create and develop a vocabulary to talk about the arts.

During work time, Liza looks at the postcards the class brought back from their field trip to the art museum the day before. She picks out all the paintings with a lot of red, and returns the rest to the basket. Liza looks intently at the red pictures for several minutes.

❖

At snacktime, Sam tells the group about going to his sister's ballet recital. "They danced a story about a princess in a sparkly dress," he says. "She fell down on the floor when the bad witch waved her wand. Then the prince jumped across the stage and saved her."

❖

At work time in the book area, Heidi looks at a book about instruments. She tells her teacher what each item is: "That's a cello. Those are the notes to play. Here's a flute and a trumpet. This is the piano. These are called the keys. They're black and white. My grandma has one. I don't know what this one is called, but it's a kind of drum."

How Art Appreciation Develops

Art appreciation is the "critical understanding and knowledge-based awareness of the meaning and aesthetics of art" (Epstein, 2005, p. 52). This concept may sound somewhat abstract and advanced for preschoolers, but in fact appreciating the arts is perfectly suited to the early childhood curriculum. With their senses open to all experiences, young children are highly aware of aesthetic features in their environment, such as the emotions evoked by color, the messages delivered through sound, the explosive energy of a movement like jumping or leaping, and the tension or playfulness of drama.

Smith et al. say the goal of art education is "to help children increase their capacity to create meaning and make sense of themselves and the world around them" (1993, p. 3). One way young children do this is to create their own art in pictures, songs, movements, and role plays. However, preschoolers can also discover meaning in the artistic creations of others, as well as the aesthetics found in nature. This process of discovery is what art appreciation is about. Children come to see that the creative arts are another way to perceive and think about the world.

The role of art appreciation in preschool education

In this country, early childhood art education typically involves making art with an emphasis on self-expression and its underlying emotions. With this focus on the affective and social value of the creative arts, preschool educators have generally overlooked art's potential to also nurture children's cognitive abilities. Howard Gardner observes that "more than any other country, art education in the United States has been considered an unimportant part of a child's scholastic profile" (1990, p. 36).

Yet, as noted earlier, art requires intellect as well as intuition (Arnheim, 1989). Thinking about an artist's intention, how a work was created, and its impact on the viewer, involves perception, memory, and concept formation. For the young child, art appreciation is highly cognitive. It entails working with principles related to color and shape, time and scale, position and direction, and pattern and sequencing. It also involves learning the language of art, and making aesthetic judgments involves reflection and critical thinking. In short, analyzing the meaning and quality of art promotes academic knowledge and skills in many other content areas. Because the creative arts enrich our personal and social lives, studying them is also valuable in and of itself.

Young children's emerging abilities in art appreciation

Research in developmental psychology (summarized in Gardner, 1990) suggests that young children are more capable of art appreciation than we give them credit for. While they are initially more likely to focus on subject matter than aesthetics, preschoolers can display a sensitivity

In this activity, children are experiencing the aesthetics of color, texture, and movement.

to the quality of artwork if adults engage them in meaningful conversation about it. Similarly, they can sort artwork on the basis of style rather than content because of their natural interest in comparing things on perceptual attributes. Children can also think about and reflect on what they see and hear. Asked open-ended questions, they can state what they think the artist is trying to say or how a work of art makes them feel.

Like any other curriculum area, young children can best engage with art appreciation when it is grounded in their own experiences and involves active, participatory learning, as in this example:

Art educator Suzanne Kolodziej (1995) describes a project in which preschoolers created their own picture museum before visiting the International Museum of Photography in Rochester, New York. The children brought in favorite photographs of themselves and gave them titles, which encouraged reflection and discussion about where and when the pictures were taken and why they were important to each child. They also labeled the photos and made a catalog with their comments. Creating the picture museum involved the children in many participatory ways. In choosing a photograph, they expressed an aesthetic preference. By describing the image, they engaged in art criticism. While creating titles, labels, and an exhibit catalog, the children acquired a sense of how museums are organized and operated. As a result, when the children later visited the museum, they had a firsthand basis for understanding the concepts of "museum" and "art collection," as well as an appreciation of photography as an art form.

Child development research, together with anecdotal accounts like the one above, indicate that young children are cognitively, linguistically, socially, and emotionally capable of appreciating art. They can regard art from the perspective of style and aesthetics, think about an artist's intentions, describe the feelings and sensations evoked by what they see and hear, and be curious about the historical and cultural forces that shape the artwork's creation. Based on these findings, preschool settings can and should support children in appreciating as well as making art.

Teaching Strategies That Support Appreciating the Arts

Preschool teacher and art educator Marjorie Schiller (1995) maintains there is no contradiction between developmentally appropriate practices and the activities associated with art criticism and art history. She finds that young children enjoy talking about art and identifying the aesthetic, personal, and social characteristics of artists and their work. To promote children's appreciation of art, music, movement, and pretend (sociodramatic) play, use the following teaching strategies.

Focus on specific aspects of artwork when you explore it with children

Young preschoolers generally pay attention to one dominant feature of a work of art, such as a bright color, fast tempo, sudden arm movement, or large prop. Even in a complex work, they tend to focus on a single aspect. As their cognitive and aesthetic abilities mature, however, older preschoolers can pay attention to an overall work and the relationship between its parts. For example, they may notice how colors play off one another, how tempos change, how arm and leg movements are coordinated, or how a plot element affects the direction of a story. To help children maintain and expand their artistic focus, always begin with the aspect that interests them, and then follow their lead as they start to notice more details and interrelationships.

At work time, several children look at postcards with reproductions of abstract paintings. Three-year-old Luke examines a picture of a Miro with large colorful shapes. Four-year-old Kelley uses her finger to trace the lines of the drips on a Jackson Pollack painting. Her teacher imitates Kelley's tracing movements with another Pollack postcard.

❖

At greeting circle, Nicholas tells his teacher about seeing a performance of the Nutcracker over the weekend. He shows her how he can "walk like a soldier" by lifting his right leg and bending his right arm, then coordinating these two movements on his left side.

❖

At small-group time, while painting to music from "Peter and the Wolf," Marie says to her teacher when the music becomes lower in pitch and shifts to a minor key, "Oh no, here comes the scary part." Her teacher acknowledges, "This music means the scary part is coming."

To begin, provide artwork with a limited number of features, such as a painting with large shapes or bold colors, an instrumental selection with a strong beat, a single body movement, or a story with a simple repetitive action. Encourage children to talk about what they observe ("What do you notice about the color?") and how it relates to them ("Do you ever move like that?"). Plan activities to help them focus on a dominant artistic element. For example, look at reproductions of work by Color Field artists, such as Mark Rothko or Helen Frankenthaler, whose paintings explore color rather than images. Listen to instrumental music so children can focus on tempo or pitch without the distraction of words. Repeat strong, dominant movements. Encourage children to act out the event (climbing into the boat) in the story they are making up.

Gradually increase the complexity of the art to encourage children to reflect on more elements. Talk about how the features relate to or affect one another. For example, comment, "I notice something different about the shapes in the middle and the shapes in the corners" or "There's a word where our voices go way up high. Let's sing the song again and listen for it." Encourage children to consider artwork from different perspectives. For example, some paintings (such as works by Seurat that feature pointillism) look like "dots" of color up close but form a complete image from farther away. Changes in body position look different when motions are viewed from the front, side, or back. Events in a story have alternative interpretations — Goldilocks enjoys her explorations of the three bears' house; the three bears regard them with dismay.

Encourage children to make and explain simple aesthetic choices

Children express aesthetic choices when they decide what color shirt to wear, make a selection from the class songbook, pick a movement for others to imitate, or choose a book to read. They also begin to show artistic preferences as they look at one painting longer than another, name their favorite song, delight in a "silly" movement, or choose to pretend play one role rather than another. However, while they may have clear preferences, younger preschoolers cannot state the reason behind them. With growing self-awareness and expanded vocabularies, older preschoolers are capable of saying why they do

Whether it's choosing colors for a painting, deciding what to wear, or making a selection from the class song book, children make aesthetic choices all day long!

(or do not) like something. They explain their choices in terms of aesthetic elements ("Yellow is a happy color"; "This music is smooth") or personal relevance ("This is how hockey players go. I'm gonna be a hockey player when I grow up" or "My grandpa says that too. It's funny!").

Create a supportive climate

As noted under general strategies, a supportive and nonjudgmental classroom climate is the single most important factor in encouraging children to take risks both creating and evaluating art. Therefore, acknowledge and comment on children's aesthetic choices rather than complimenting or praising them. For example, you might say, "You chose the painting with lots of blue," rather than "Blue is my favorite color." It's fine to express your own preferences as long as it is clear you are not disagreeing with theirs. So, for example, you might say, "Maribel likes to kick her legs high in the air. I enjoy gliding smoothly across the floor. And Jonah has fun spinning in a circle until he gets dizzy!"

Provide a variety of artistic materials and styles

To help children become aware of what and why aesthetic attributes appeal to them, provide a wide variety of artistic materials and styles so they can find something they are drawn to. For example, offer visual art in different 2-dimensional and 3-dimensional media (painting, ink drawing, collage, pottery, weaving, carving, photography). Play instrumental music in different styles. Sing songs that are serious and songs that are funny (preschoolers are beginning to enjoy humor). Also offer a wide range of options in other areas of the creative arts.

Provide language for talking about the arts

Finally, as you provide children with a language for talking about the arts (see general strategies and suggestions that follow), encourage them to use that vocabulary in describing their aesthetic preferences. Talk about what appeals to them in terms of color, form, or line. Describe the tickle in your throat of singing deep down or the pleasurable sensation of sliding your voice up the scale to its highest note. Encourage children to label their facial gestures or body movements, and explain the joy of meeting the physical challenges they set for themselves. Talk about what makes a story worth reading, such as the thrill of suspense or the reassuring predictability of a character's behavior.

At work time in the book area, Hazel looks at the book An Eye for Color: The Story of Josef Albers *by Natasha Wing. When she points to a painting with a large orange square, her teacher Adele comments that it "glows with warmth." Hazel says it looks like a blanket.*

❖

At small-group time, while reading the book Rosie's Walk *by Pat Hutchins, the children wonder aloud whether the fox will catch Rosie the hen. "What do you think?" asks Carlos, their teacher. The children say they don't know and turn the page. "This book has a lot of suspense," Carlos says. "It keeps us wondering what will happen next!"*

Discuss the feelings expressed through artwork

Young children may be aware of the feelings an artist is trying to convey, although they may not be able to express them in words (similar to recognizing but not being able to explain their own aesthetic choices). As their verbal abilities increase — especially their vocabulary for describing emotions — preschoolers become more adept at identifying and describing these elements in a work of art. For example, they can say whether a line drawing is happy or sad, a piece of music sounds busy, a movement conveys being tired, or a dramatic incident is scary. Children can also represent the underlying emotion of a work of art through their own facial expressions, gestures, and whole body movements, for example, by frowning or slumping to express sadness or hopping with glee.

Making art is an excellent way for children to express emotions. Responding to artwork can also reassure them and help them understand that others share their feelings. The creative arts are an especially potent vehicle for children with limited verbal skills who can sense but not yet articulate the emotional content of a piece of art. You can provide these children with opportunities to represent the feelings portrayed in art in other ways. For example, they might make a drawing (choose dark blue for "sad"), sing a simple melody (use a high pitch for "happy"), tap out a beat (pat a slow tempo for "suspenseful"), or gesture expressively during pretend play (put their hands to their mouths to show they are "scared").

Older preschoolers, who are increasingly able to take another person's perspective, are also able to say what they believe an artist was thinking or feeling while creating a work of art. Likewise, they can articulate the emotions that art evokes in them. To support this development, comment on the emotional content of art yourself. For example, you might say, "This pale green looks soothing, like a soft baby blanket." Use descriptive language in your daily conversations with children: "Whenever I wear this shiny red dress, it makes me so happy I want to dance!"

Luke observes the big, bold strokes in a landscape depicting the Old West and comments that the artist "was really excited about painting galloping horses!"

❖

Nicole lowers her head and folds her arms across her face. "This is my sad move," she explains to her teacher Tom. Then she thrusts her head up and lifts her arms over her head. "When I'm glad, I go like this! Like when my cousin Cynthia visits me."

Describing the feelings expressed in their own art helps children do the same for the work of others, much like talking about their own feelings helps them develop empathy. Words provide a point of recognition and the language to make comparisons. Talk with children about their creations as a lead-in to discussing an artist's intentions. Encourage parents to do the same. When you display or send children's artwork home, or they demonstrate a movement for parents, help children share the feelings behind these creations with family members.

At pick-up time, Mrs. Whelan reminds Sloan to get the picture from his cubby. As Sloan hands it to his mom, Mrs. Whelan tells her, "Today we read a book about a boy who was nervous about his first day of school, and Sloan made this drawing." As Sloan's mother looks at it, Mrs. Whelan comments on the many dark, hastily-drawn lines criss-crossing the paper. "You were scared the first day of school too," his mother says to Sloan. "Yes," he agrees, "but not anymore."

Making music is one of the ways children express their emotions and their aesthetic perceptions.

❖

At large-group time, Ilyon makes swimming motions with her arms. Earlier in the day, she had talked about seeing the movie "Finding Nemo" with her cousins. Her teacher comments, "You are moving like a fish." Ilyon replies, "That's how Nemo swam when he was trying to get away from the bad guys. He was scared they would catch him, and he missed his daddy."

Finally, give children time to study and absorb the feelings conveyed in works of art. Play several minutes of a piece of music and repeat it over several days; extend and repeat a movement activity so children can practice and master a skill enough to try variations; talk about the characters' emotions in familiar books; and refrain from rushing children as they linger over illustrations in a familiar book. Children may not initially pay attention to the emotions on their own, but by intentionally providing opportunities for them to do so, appreciating arts' affective components will become an established part of their observational and conversational skills.

Expose children to the materials, tools, and techniques used by artists

Although children often encounter visual images and music, they may be unaware of the artistry in what they see and hear. Moreover, there are many areas of art (an orchestra, dance, or theater performance) that children are unlikely to encounter at all without a conscious effort on the part of parents and teachers. Children are therefore highly dependent on adults to facilitate their art appreciation by offering children a wide variety of artistic media, and a range of materials, techniques, and styles within each medium.

This teacher introduces children to the style and technique of the painter Picasso.

The following strategies will help raise preschoolers' awareness of and interest in the breadth and depth of the creative arts:

- *Art* — Illustrated storybooks present artwork done in different styles (realistic and abstract, simple and complex, color and black and white) and many types of media (paint, pen and ink, photographs, collage). Once children are familiar with the pictures and story, elicit their thoughts about the artwork and talk together about the media used to create it. Find books about artists and their work written specifically for preschool-age children, and/or focus on the photos in adult art books. Bring in reproductions of fine art, such as postcards and posters, and encourage conversation about the materials, techniques, and styles used by the artists. Include examples of painting, sculpture, ceramics, fiber, beads, collage, wood, metal, photography, architecture, landscape design, and so on. Explore the range of subject matter and the feelings represented in these types of visual art.

- *Music* — During large-group time, play musical selections that feature many different types of live and recorded music. In addition to albums created especially for preschoolers, be sure children hear classical, jazz, opera, folk songs, and other genres. Play music from around the world. Explain that music is created by composers. Provide pictures (album covers or concert posters) so children can see that music is made by individuals, duos, small groups, choirs, bands, and orchestras. Offer a variety of simple percussion and string instruments for children to play, and search out opportunities for them to hear and see other music-makers from around the world.

- *Movement* — Take advantage of the variety in other art forms as a springboard for exploring the range of creative movement. For example, as children move to music, discuss how their bodies respond to its tonal quality, tempo, or pitch. Encourage them to move in ways inspired by the properties of visual art, such as size, color, shape, line, and mood. Preschoolers should not be plunked down in front of the DVD player, but you can look for images, such as those in photo books, that illustrate dance styles and performance settings from around the world.

- *Pretend play* — Movies and television are a pervasive part of young children's lives today. You can use children's interest in these dramatic sources as a springboard for more diverse and active learning. For example, they may develop a play theme at work time based on a favorite movie or show. To help children move beyond repeating scripted lines and to encourage more complex play, add related materials, enter as a partner in their play, and provide real-life experiences (such as visitors and field trips, described in the next section) to broaden their interests and knowledge. Here is a statement from a HighScope staff member who tried these techniques when she became uneasy with children's unimaginative "superhero" play:

I found that as I used these strategies, I became more comfortable with superhero play in my setting. I realized that it made sense to approach children's play with power characters just as I would any other form of pretending. What would I do if a child were pretending to drive to Georgia, to be a kitty, to be a baby, or to be Batman?

My response would be the same: to support and encourage the play, regardless of its theme. As I became more relaxed with superhero play and allowed it to grow and develop, I could see its richness and complexity (Marshall, 2001, pp. 51–52).

Plan local field trips to introduce children to the creative arts

Look for arts venues in your community — studios, galleries, performance spaces — that welcome young children and can accommodate their active learning. For example, a growing number of museums have "hands-on" opportunities for children to see art up close. Art fairs, botanical gardens, landscaped parks, statues, and monuments also offer settings where young children can actively view art. Some communities have programs (for example, those sponsored by Wolf Trap Foundation for the Performing Arts) that pay for performing artists, such as musicians, to come into the classroom. You can take preschoolers on field trips to hear live musical performances, such as choir, band, and orchestra concerts at schools or civic performances, that are specifically arranged for young children. Look for informal opportunities as well, for example, the street performances of musicians or dancers during a nearby farmer's market or an outdoor art fair. An increasing number of community theater groups also stage performances specifically for young audiences, keeping in mind both the appropriate length and content that will hold their interest.

In preparing for classroom visits and field trips, learn as much as possible beforehand about the people and places involved. Talk with parents, artists, and docents about the children's interests. Help them understand what preschoolers are likely to say and do so they will be ready to work with them. Foreknowledge of the upcoming experience will also help you plan prior activities that will make the visit or performance more meaningful to the children. For example, if a ceramics artist is visiting the classroom, plan to use clay at several small-group times and provide books and art magazines with pictures of pottery. If the class will be attending a play based on a classic children's story, read it out loud several times before the performance.

Also look for ways to extend these experiences afterward. Encourage children to represent the visit or field trip itself through a variety of media and group writing activities. When possible, encourage parents and artists to leave materials that the children can use to carry out the same type of artistic endeavor (such as yarn, clay, carving tools, CDs, dance posters, theater programs, used tickets). Add related materials to the classroom to further help children represent and extend their experiences (empty cartons, socks, and yarn if children want to re-create a puppet show). Finally, let people know how much you and the children value their contributions. Take dictation for a collective "thank you" letter. Send photos and samples of how children demonstrate their excitement about the experience and incorporate what they learned in their daily play.

For illustrations of how children engage in appreciating the arts, and the ways adults can support and incrementally extend their capacity for art appreciation, see "Ideas for Scaffolding KDI. 44 Appreciating the Arts" on page 92. The suggestions presented in the chart offer additional ideas to help you play and interact with children in many different ways throughout the daily routine.

Ideas for Scaffolding KDI 44. Appreciating the Arts

Always support children at their current level and occasionally offer a gentle extension.

Earlier	Middle	Later
Children may • Choose without expressing an aesthetic preference; not state a like or dislike (e.g., pick the song on the first page of the song book; paint with blue because it's the color closest to them on the table). • Observe or participate in the creative arts without paying attention to its artistic elements (e.g., look at a picture without commenting on its shapes or colors).	*Children may* • Express an aesthetic preference but not be able to say why they do (or do not) like something (e.g., "I like the purple one"; "Twinkle, Twinkle is my favorite song"). • Describe one artistic element such as color or tempo (e.g., "It's red"; "That's fast music"); focus on the content rather than the style of the art (e.g., "It's a picture of a dog"; "Effie's pretending to skate").	*Children may* • State a reason for their aesthetic preference (e.g., "Blue is my best color because it's like the lake where daddy taught me to swim"; "Not that book. The pictures are too scary! I like this one. The pictures are silly!"). • Describe several artistic features in terms of style and content (e.g., "It's a red circle with fuzzy edges"); say what their own artwork expresses (e.g., "This music makes me angry so I'm stomping").
To support children's current level, adults can • Accept that children may not have an aesthetic preference (e.g., "You like all three poems"). • Provide a variety of interesting artwork for children to look at and musical selections to listen to.	*To support children's current level, adults can* • Validate children's aesthetic choices without making judgments or comparisons (e.g., "Some of us like to move to fast music and others prefer moving to slow music"). • Show interest in whatever artistic element catches the child's attention (e.g., "That is a big green square in the middle!"; "This music sure is fast!"; "Let's try to copy that movement together").	*To support children's current level, adults can* • Acknowledge the reasons for children's preferences (e.g., "You like books with silly, not scary, pictures"). • Ask children to describe the content and style of their artwork (e.g., "Tell me about the lines you drew"; "What do you call it when you move that way?").
To offer a gentle extension, adults can • Expose children to many artistic styles in a wide range of media so they can discover if/what they like. • Comment on an observable characteristic of artwork or a noticeable difference in music (e.g., "There's a lot of yellow in this painting"; "This music is slow").	*To offer a gentle extension, adults can* • Say why you do (not) like something (e.g., "I like this music. It makes me feel happy"); encourage children to say why they do (not) like something (e.g., "What makes you say this picture is yucky?"). • Refer children to one another to share observations (e.g., "Jeremy is looking at the same photo. I wonder what he sees").	*To offer a gentle extension, adults can* • Provide a variety of artwork so children can find other examples of qualities they like (e.g., art reproductions; books by the same illustrator; music in similar genres). • Expand children's vocabulary to describe materials, tools, techniques, and styles (e.g., "When the music is jumpy like this, it's called 'staccato'"); encourage them to describe what others are expressing in their artwork (e.g., "Why do you think the artist drew all these busy lines?").

Creative Arts: A Summary

General teaching strategies that support creative arts

- Provide open-ended art materials[5] and experiences.
- Establish a climate that supports creative risk-taking and emphasizes process over product.
- Encourage children to represent real and imaginary experiences through the arts.
- Talk with children about the arts.
- Draw on the artistic forms in the cultures of children's families and communities.

Teaching strategies that support art

- Provide diverse examples of visual art throughout the learning environment.
- Give children time to explore art materials and tools in depth.
- Display and send home children's artwork.

Teaching strategies that support music

- Look for opportunities to listen to, identify, and create sounds with children.
- Sing with children.
- Play a wide variety of recorded and live music.
- Provide simple instruments.

Teaching strategies that support movement

- Describe and encourage children to describe their creative use of movement.
- Encourage children to solve movement problems at group times and transitions.
- Provide opportunities for children to represent their experiences through movement.
- Encourage simple ways of moving creatively to music.

Teaching strategies that support pretend play

- Support children as they imitate what they see and hear.
- Watch for and support imaginative role play throughout the classroom.
- Participate as a partner in children's pretend play.

Teaching strategies that support appreciating the arts

- Focus on specific aspects of artwork when you explore it with children.
- Encourage children to make and explain simple aesthetic choices.
- Discuss the feelings expressed through artwork.
- Expose children to the materials, tools, and techniques used by artists.
- Plan local field trips to introduce children to the creative arts.

[5]Program staff should adhere to their state's licensing regulations when adding materials to the classroom. Check local licensing regulations and agencies and organizations such as the Consumer Product Safety Commission (www.cpsc.gov), the American Academy of Pediatrics (www.aap.org), and the National Resource Center for Health and Safety in Child Care and Early Education (www.nrckids.org) for current information on product safety.

References

Althouse, R., Johnson, M. H., & Mitchell, S. T. (2003). *The colors of learning: Integrating the visual arts into the early childhood curriculum.* New York, NY: Teachers College Press.

Americans for the Arts. (2010, August 23). Keeping the arts alive, even in a recession. Retrieved from http://www.artsusa.org

Arnheim, R. (1989). *Thoughts on art education.* Los Angeles, CA: Getty Center for Education in the Arts.

Arts Education Partnership. (1998). *Young children and the arts: Making creative connections — A report of the Task Force on Children's Learning and the Arts: Birth to age eight.* Washington, DC: Author.

Beatty, B. (1995). *Preschool education in America.* New Haven: Yale University Press.

Bodrova, E., & Leong, D. (2007). *Tools of the mind: The Vygotskian approach to early childhood education* (2nd ed.). New York, NY: Prentice Hall.

Bronson, P., & Merryman, A. (2010, July 10). The creativity crisis. *Newsweek.* Retrieved from www.newsweek.com/2010/07/10/the-creativity-crisis.print.html

Brownell, C. A. (1990). Peer social skills in toddlers: Competencies and constraints illustrated by same-age and mixed-age interaction. *Child Development, 61,* 838-848.

Centers for Disease Control. (2010). *The association between school-based physical activity, including physical education, and academic performance.* Atlanta, GA: US Department of Health and Human Services.

Chafel, J. A. (1984). "Call the police, okay?" Social comparison by young children during play in preschool. *Early Child Development and Care, 14,* 201–216.

Chenfield, M. B. (2005). Education is a moving experience: Get movin'! In D. Koralek (Ed.), *Spotlight on young children and the creative arts* (pp. 50–51). Washington, DC: National Association for the Education of Young Children.

Cole, D., & LaVoie, J. C. (1985). Fantasy play and related cognitive development in 2- to 6-year-olds. *Developmental Psychology, 21*(20), 233–240. doi:10.1037//0012-1649.21.2.233

Copple, C., & Bredekamp, S. (Eds.). (2009). *Developmentally appropriate practice in early childhood programs serving children from birth through age 8* (3rd ed.).Washington, DC: National Association for the Education of Young Children.

Creasey, G. L., Jarvis, P. A., & Berk, L. E. (1998). Play and social competence. In O. N. Saracho & B. Spodek (Eds.), *Multiple perspectives on play in early childhood education* (pp. 116–143). Albany, NY: State University of New York.

Dobbs, S. M. (1998). *Learning in and through art.* Los Angeles, CA: Getty Education Institute for the Arts.

Drew, W. F., & Rankin, B. (2005). In D. Koralek (Ed.), *Spotlight on young children and the creative arts* (pp. 32–39). Washington, DC: National Association for the Education of Young Children.

Epstein, A. S. (2005). Thinking about art: Encouraging art appreciation in early childhood settings. In D. Koralek (Ed.). (2005). *Spotlight on young children and the creative arts* (pp. 52–57). Washington, DC: National Association for the Education of Young Children.

Epstein, A. S. (2007). *The intentional teacher: Choosing the best strategies for young children's learning.* Washington, DC: National Association for the Education of Young Children.

Epstein, A. S. (2012). *Langugage, Literacy, and Communication.* Ypsilanti, MI: HighScope Press.

Epstein, A. S., & Hohmann, M. (2012). *The HighScope Preschool Curriculum.* Ypsilanti, MI: HighScope Press.

Epstein, A. S., & Trimis, E. (2002). *Supporting young artists: The development of the visual arts in young children.* Ypsilanti, MI: HighScope Press.

Fiske, E. B. (Ed.). (1999). *Champions of change: The impact of the arts on learning.* Washington, DC: Arts Education Partnership and the President's Committee on the Arts and Humanities.

Fromberg, D. (1999). A review of research on play. In C. Seefeldt (Ed.), *The early childhood curriculum: Current findings in theory and practice* (pp. 27–53). New York, NY: Teachers College Press.

Gardner, H. (1982). *Art, mind, and brain.* New York, NY: Basic Books.

Gardner, H. (1990). *Art education and human development.* Los Angeles, CA: Getty Center for Education in the Arts.

Goleman, D., Kaufman, P., & Ray, M. (1993). *The creative spirit.* New York, NY: Plume.

Goodenough, F. L. (1926). *Children's drawings as measures of intellectual maturity.* New York, NY: Harcourt Brace.

Gordon, E. E. (1989). *Learning sequences in music.* Chicago, IL: G.I.A. Publications.

Haraksin-Probst, L., Hutson-Brandhagen, J., & Weikart, P. S. (2008). *Making connections: Movement, music, and literacy.* Ypsilanti, MI: HighScope Press.

Hargreaves, D. J., & Zimmerman, P. F. (1992). Developmental theories of music learning. In R. Cowell (Ed.), *Handbook of research on music teaching and learning* (pp. 377–391). New York, NY: Schirmer.

Kavanaugh, R. D. (2006). Pretend play. In B. Spodek & O. N. Saracho (Eds.), *Handbook of research on the education of young children* (2nd ed., pp. 269–278). Mahwah, NJ: Lawrence Erlbaum.

Kemple, K. M., Batey, J. J., & Hartle, L. C. (2005). Music play: Creating centers for musical play and exploration. In D. Koralek (Ed.), *Spotlight on young children and the creative arts* (pp. 24–31). Washington, DC: National Association for the Education of Young Children.

Kerlavage, M. S. (1995). A bunch of naked ladies and a tiger: Children's responses to adult works of art. In C. M. Thompson (Ed.), *The visual arts and early childhood learning* (pp. 56–62). Reston, VA: National Art Education Association.

Kindler, A. M. (1995). Significance of adult input in early childhood artistic development. In C. M. Thompson (Ed.), *The visual arts and early childhood learning* (pp. 1–5). Reston, VA: National Art Education Association.

Kolodziej, S. (1995). The picture museum: Creating a photography museum with children. In C. M. Thompson (Ed.), *The visual arts and early childhood learning* (pp. 52–55). Reston, VA: National Art Education Association.

Koralek, D. (2005). Spotlight on young children and the creative arts. In D. Koralek (Ed.), *Spotlight on young children and the creative arts* (pp. 2–3). Washington, DC: National Association for the Education of Young Children.

Lowenfeld, V. (1947). *Creative and mental growth.* New York, NY: Macmillan.

Marshall, B. (1992). *"Want your hair cut?" Strategies for increasing children's representational play.* Unpublished master's thesis. Oakland University, Rochester, MI.

Marshall, B. (2001). Ban it, ignore it, or join it? What to do about superhero play. In N. A. Brickman (Ed.), *Supporting young learners,* (Vol. 3, pp. 43–52). Ypsilanti, MI: HighScope Press.*

Matlock, R., & Hornstein, J. (2005). Saber-toothed tiger: Learning and the arts through the ages. In D. Koralek (Ed.), *Spotlight on young children and the creative arts* (pp. 6–11). Washington, DC: National Association for the Education of Young Children.

McMahon, O. (1987). An exploration of aesthetic awareness in preschool age children. *Bulletin of the Council for Research in Music Education, 91,* 97–102.

Metz, E. (1989). Movement as a musical response among preschool children. *Journal of Research in Music Education, 37*(1), 48–60. doi:10.2307/3344952

Moorhead, G., & Pond, D. (1941/1978). *Music for young children.* Santa Barbara, CA: Pillsbury Foundation for the Advancement of Music Education.

Paley, V. (1990). *The boy who would be a helicopter.* Cambridge, MA: Harvard University Press.

Parsons, M. J. (1987). *How we understand art.* Cambridge, England: Cambridge University Press.

Piaget, J. (1951/1962). *Play, dreams, and imitation in childhood.* New York, NY: Norton.

Praisner, D. (1984). Artist's drawing. *Studies in Art Education, 22*(2), 34–43.

Sawyers, K. S. (with Colley, E., & Icaza, L.). (2010). *Moving with purpose: 54 activities for learning, fitness, and fun.* Ypsilanti, MI: HighScope Press.

Schiller, M. (1995). An emergent art curriculum that fosters understanding. *Young Children, 50*(3), 33–38.

Scott-Kasner, C. (1992). Research on music in early childhood. In R. Colwell (Ed.), *Handbook of research on music teaching and learning* (pp. 633–650). Reston, VA: Music Educators National Conference.

Seefeldt, C. (1995). Art — A serious work. *Young Children, 50*(3), 39–45.

*Also available at the HighScope *Extensions* archive at highscope.org.

Seefeldt, C. (1999). Art for young children. In C. Seefeldt (Ed.), *The early childhood curriculum: Current findings in theory and practice* (3rd ed., pp. 201–217). New York, NY: Teachers College Press.

Sims, W. L. (1985). Young children's creative movement to music: Categories of movement, rhythmic characteristics, and reactions to change. *Contributions to Music Education, 12*, 42–50.

Sims, W. L. (1991). Research on music listening in early childhood. *Music in Early Childhood: A Research Journal*, 1(1), 5–7.

Smith, N. R. (with Fucigna, C., Kennedy, M., & Lord, L.). (1993). *Experience and art: Teaching children to paint* (2nd ed.). New York, NY: Teachers College Press.

Stellaccio, C. K., & McCarthy, M. (1999). Research in early childhood music and movement education. In C. Seefeldt (Ed.), *The early childhood curriculum: Current findings in theory and practice* (3rd ed., pp. 179–200). New York, NY: Teachers College Press.

Tarnowski, S. M., & Leclerc, J. (1994). Musical play of preschoolers and teacher-child interaction. *Update, Applications of Research in Music Education, 13*(1), 9–16.

Taunton, M., & Colbert, M. (2000). Art in the early childhood classroom: Authentic experiences and extended dialogues. In N. J. Yelland (Ed.), *Promoting meaningful learning: Innovation in educating early childhood professionals* (pp. 67–76). Washington, DC: National Association for the Education of Young Children.

Thompson, C. M. (1995). Transforming curriculum in the visual arts. In S. Bredekamp & T. Rosegrant (Eds.), *Reaching potentials: Transforming early childhood curriculum and assessment* (Vol. 2, pp. 81–96). Washington, DC: National Association for the Education of Young Children.

Tomlinson, H. B., & Hyson, M. (2009). Developmentally appropriate practice in the preschool years — ages 3–5: An overview. In C. Copple & S. Bredekamp (Eds.), *Developmentally appropriate practice in early childhood programs serving children from birth through age 8* (3rd ed., pp. 111–148). Washington, DC: National Association for the Education of Young Children.

Vygotsky, L. (1978). *Mind and society: The development of higher psychological processes*. Cambridge, MA: Harvard University Press.

Weikart, P. S. (2000). *Round the circle: Key experiences in movement for young children*. Ypsilanti, MI: HighScope Press.

Wolf, D., & Perry, M. D. (1989). From endpoints to repertoires. *Journal of Aesthetic Education, 22*, 17–34. doi:10.2307/3332961